ISBN 978-1-330-94001-3
PIBN 10124039

1 MONTH OF
FREE
READING

at

www.ForgottenBooks.com

By purchasing this book you are eligible for one month membership to ForgottenBooks.com, giving you unlimited access to our entire collection of over 700,000 titles via our web site and mobile apps.

To claim your free month visit:

www.forgottenbooks.com/free124039

Similar Books Are Available from
www.forgottenbooks.com

SCHOOL MANAGEMENT:

INCLUDING A FULL DISCUSSION OF

3263

School Economy, School Ethics, School Government,

AND THE

PROFESSIONAL RELATIONS OF THE TEACHER.

DESIGNED FOR USE BOTH AS A TEXTBOOK AND AS A BOOK OF REFER-
ENCE FOR TEACHERS, PARENTS AND SCHOOL OFFICERS.

BY

A. N. RAUB, A.M., Ph.D.,

*President of Delaware College, Newark, Del , and Author of "Lessons
in English," "Practical English Grammar," "Practical
Rhetoric," "Studies in English and American
Literature," "Methods of Teaching," etc.*

PHILADELPHIA:
R A U B & C O.
1889.

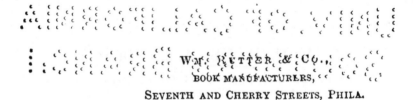

WM. RETTER & CO.,
BOOK MANUFACTURERS,
SEVENTH AND CHERRY STREETS, PHILA.

WESTCOTT & THOMSON,
Stereotypers and Electrotypers, Philada.

PREFACE.

THE Author of this book believes that teaching is a science based on principles as firmly fixed, as readily determined, and capable of being as thoroughly systematized, as those of either law, medicine, or theology.

He believes, also, that teaching is destined to rank among the foremost of the learned professions, and that, considered with reference to the magnitude and importance of the work to be accomplished, this profession is inferior to no other.

He believes, therefore, in the necessity of special preparation for this calling as for other important callings in life, and that no one should assume the duties and responsibilities incident to teaching without a knowledge of the human body, the functions of the physical organs, and the laws of health, as well as a knowledge of the human mind, its faculties, and the methods of their development and culture. He holds, also, that the teacher should have a thorough knowledge of the best methods of management, as well as be entirely familiar with the most valuable methods of instruction and culture. Without this knowledge the teacher can be only an experimenter who works at random; with it, he is prepared to win success and aid in elevating his calling to the dignity which should characterize it as a profession.

It is the object of this book to discuss briefly, but as thoroughly as possible, the subject of School Management—including School Requisites; School Organization, both temporary and permanent; School Work, its objects and the means of securing the best results; School Ethics; School Government; and the Professional Relations of the Teacher,—a knowledge of all of which is necessary to successful professional teaching.

Want of a knowledge of good management is a prolific source of failure in school work; and such knowledge is, therefore, specially important to the teacher.

This book aims to include the principles on which has been based the successful experience of the best teachers of this and other countries, so arranged as to make the information available not only in the class-room, but also to the private student, whether teacher, parent, or school officer.

The Author advocates no untried theories. His aim is to impart information such as is deemed valuable to all who have control of children. He offers only such suggestions as have been found valuable in practice, and points out the faults and mistakes which his observation has convinced him are the most frequent causes of failure. He sincerely hopes that the book may prove specially valuable to every earnest teacher desirous of success in his calling.

A. N. R.

STATE NORMAL SCHOOL, LOCK HAVEN, PA.,
Aug. 24, 1882.

CONTENTS.

PAGE

INTRODUCTION 11

CHAPTER I.

SCHOOL REQUISITES.

I. SCHOOL-HOUSES 13
   1. *The Location* 14
      1. Healthfulness of the Site 14
      2. Convenience of Access 15
      3. Quiet 16
      4. Beauty 16
   2. *The Size and Proportions* 17
   3. *The Architecture* 17
   4. *Internal Arrangement* 18
II. ARRANGEMENT AND SIZE OF THE GROUNDS 20
   1. *Size* 21
   2. *Convenience of Arrangement* 21
   3. *Beauty of the Grounds* 21
   4. *Appurtenances* 22
III. SCHOOL FURNITURE AND APPARATUS 23
   1. *Desks* 23
   2. *Blackboard* 23
   3. *Erasers* 24
   4. *Pointers* 24
   5. *Reading-Charts* 25
   6. *Numeral Frame* 25
   7. *Geographical Apparatus* 25
   8. *Cabinets* 26
   9. *Dictionary* 26
      How to Secure Apparatus 26

PAGE

IV. SCHOOL HYGIENE . . . . , . . 27
 1. *Lighting* 28
 2. *Heating* 29
 3. *Ventilation* 31
 4. *Condition of Floors and Walls* 33
 5. *Posture of Pupils* 34
 6. *Exercise* 35
 7. *Play* 36
 8. *Hygienic Habits of Pupils* 39
  Suggestions on School Hygiene 42

V. SCHOOL GRADES 43
 1. *Advantages* 44
 2. *Objection to Graded Schools* 46
 3. *The Number of Grades* 46
 4. *Manner of Grading* 47
 5. *The Kindergarten* 49

VI. SCHOOL AIDS 49
 1. *Textbooks* 50
  1. The Objects of Textbooks 50
  2. The Characteristics of Good Textbooks . 51
  3. The Abuse of Textbooks 54
  4. The Selection of Textbooks 55
  5. The Ownership of Textbooks 56
 2. *The School Library* 56
 3. *School Records* 58

CHAPTER II.

SCHOOL ORGANIZATION.

PERMANENT ORGANIZATION 66
1. *School Classification* 66
 Advantages of Classification 67
 Principles of Classification 68
2. *Programme* 72
 Characteristics of a Good Programme . 72
 Advantages of a Good Programme 74
3. *School Signals* 77

PAGE
4. *Hand Signals* 79
5. *The Opening and the Closing of School* 80
6. *Seating* 82
7. *Recesses* 82

CHAPTER III.

SCHOOL WORK.

I. STUDY 85
  1. *The Objects of Study* 85
    1. Discipline 85
    2. The Acquisition of Knowledge 86
    3. Expertness 87
    4. Moral Culture 88
    5. Aspiration 88
  2. *Conditions of Successful Study* 89
  3. *Helps to Study* 90
  4. *Incentives to Study* 91
    Proper Incentives 91
    Unwise Incentives 97
  5. *How to Study* 103
  6. *Attention* 105
  7. *Rules for Study* 109
II. RECITATION 111
  1. *Objects of the Recitation* 111
  2. *Methods of Recitation* 115
    1. The Socratic Method 116
    2. The Topical Method 117
    3. The Question Method 118
    4. The Discussion Method 119
    5. The Conversational Method 120
    6. The Oral or Lecture Method 121
  3. *The Art of Questioning* 122
    1. Objects of Questioning 122
    2. How to Put Questions 124
    3. The Subject-Matter of Questions 126
    4. The Form of Questions 127
    5. The Manner of Putting Questions . 128

PAGE

4. *Answer* 128
5. *Criticism* 130
6. *Preparation for the Recitation* 131
   1. The Teacher's Preparation 131
   2. The Pupil's Preparation 133
7. *The Teacher in the Recitation* 134
8. *The Pupil in the Recitation* 137

III. EXAMINATIONS 138
1. *Objects of Examinations* 138
2. *Scope of the Examination* 139
3. *Frequency of Examinations* 141
4. *Method of Examining* 142
5. *Length of Examinations* 143

IV. REVIEWS 144
Frequency of Reviews 145

V. SCHOOL REPORTS 146

VI. GRADUATION IN PUBLIC SCHOOLS 149
Examination for Graduation 151

VII. A COURSE OF STUDY FOR COUNTRY SCHOOLS . 152

CHAPTER IV.

SCHOOL ETHICS.

1. *Duties of the Teacher* 153
   1. To Pupils 153
   2. To the Community 157
   3. To his Profession 160
   4. To Himself 165
2. *Duties of Pupils* 166
3. *Duties of School Officers* 167
4. *Duties of the Superintendent* 169

CHAPTER V.

SCHOOL GOVERNMENT.

1. *Objects of School Government* 171
2. *School Control* 173

PAGE

3. *Elements of Governing Power* 173
4. *Causes of Disorder* 185
5. *Means of Avoiding Disorder* 191
6. *Rules and Regulations* 196
7. *School Punishments* 200
    1. Objects of School Punishment 200
    2. Principles Governing Punishment 201
    3. The Degree of Punishment 203
    4. Kinds of Punishment 206
        1. Judicious Punishments 206
        2. Injudicious Punishments 223
8. *How to Detect Offenders* 225
9. *The Self-Reporting System* 228
10. *Pardons* 229
11. *Punishment of Offenses* 231

CHAPTER VI.

THE TEACHER.

1. *The Teacher's Physical Qualifications* 243
2. *The Teacher's Intellectual Qualifications* 245
3. *The Teacher's Professional Qualifications* 248
4. *The Teacher's Moral Qualifications* 254
5. *Faults to be Avoided by Teacher* 262

SCHOOL MANAGEMENT.

INTRODUCTION.

SCHOOL MANAGEMENT is that department of educational science which treats of the management and control of schools. It includes not only school economy proper, but also school government and school ethics. It has for its object the regulation of all school work in such a manner as will meet the true end of education in training the children of the land to be not only good citizens, but also symmetrically-developed men and women in an intellectual and a moral as well as a physical sense.

School management and *methods of instruction* are to some extent interwoven and dependent, and the teacher who is successful in one is usually successful in the other, because the same principles in a great measure underlie both, and the same personal qualities characterize to a great degree the faithful, energetic teacher and the successful disciplinarian.

11

The chief topics to be discussed under the subject of school management are—

1. SCHOOL REQUISITES.
2. SCHOOL ORGANIZATION.
3. SCHOOL WORK.
4. SCHOOL ETHICS.
5. SCHOOL GOVERNMENT.
6. THE TEACHER.

CHAPTER I.

School Requisites.

Previous to the organization of the school there is a certain amount of preparation necessary in order that the school work may be well done. Among the requisites demanding attention are the following:

I. School-Houses.
II. Arrangement and Size of the Grounds.
III. School Furniture.
IV. School Hygiene.
V. School Grades.
VI. School Aids.

I. School-Houses.

One of the first things to be considered in school management is the school-house. The influence exerted on the pupils, on the teacher, and on the community by either a good or a poor school-house can hardly be estimated. A good school-house, properly located, beautified as it should be, and made comfortable, pleasant, and inviting, is in itself a teacher for good; while a neglected one, the reverse of all this, does an incalculable amount of harm in counteracting efficient teaching and in moulding for evil the character of a whole neighborhood.

The chief points to be considered in connection with school-houses are the following:

1. **The Location.**
2. **The Size and Proportions.**
3. **The Architecture.**
4. **The Internal Arrangement.**

1. The Location.—The proper location of a school-house is a matter of much importance. It must be remembered that here, in a great measure, is moulded the character of the future men and women of the country. Here the tastes are cultivated and the habits formed which are to mark the future citizens. Here not only the intellectual, but also the moral and the physical, nurture are to be given.

Among the chief considerations which should determine the location of a school-house in any district are the following :

1. Healthfulness of the Site.
2. Convenience of Access.
3. Quiet.
4. Beauty.

1. Healthfulness of the Site.—It is evident that no school-house should be located where pupils are placed in danger of contracting disease. No school-house, therefore, should be built near a swamp or near stagnant water, where malarial or miasmatic vapors may endanger the health of both pupils and teacher. Nor should a school-house in a town or a city be so located as to endanger the health of its occupants by causing them to breathe the gases and effluvia arising from improperly drained streets, neighboring stables, or leaky and defective sewers. Every precaution should be taken to select the most healthful spot in the neighborhood, that the physical welfare of the children may not be jeoparded.

A sloping hillside, where the surface drainage is good, is an excellent location for a school-house, particularly if the grounds can be so arranged as to have the house face to the south or the east. If such a site can be found, with a briskly-flowing brook at the foot of the hill, it will be all the more desirable.

Expense should be no consideration. The most healthful location is not too good nor too expensive when the physical nurture of our children is to be provided for. The school law of Pennsylvania, and possibly that of other States, gives to School Boards the power to select whatever site they may see fit, providing always that a reasonable sum is paid to the landowner for the land thus appropriated.

2. **Convenience of Access.**—The second important consideration in the location of a school-house is convenience of access. In general, the school-house should be located at such place as will make it convenient for the greatest number, provided a healthful location can be secured. But the question of healthfulness should be the first to claim the attention of those having the power to locate school-buildings. In sparsely populated districts the location should usually be near the centre of the district, but where the population is dense and the distance to be traveled not so great, any location may be selected that meets the requirements of health and comfort. In the location of houses for primary pupils care should be taken that the building be so placed that as few as possible may be required to cross railways, canals, streams, or much-traveled streets.

3. Quiet.—Few appreciate the value of quiet surroundings so highly as does the student. School-houses should be so located as to afford the best possible opportunity for study. The location should be such that no noise or outside excitement may attract the attention of the pupils or divert it from its proper object. School-houses should therefore never be located near noisy manufactories, railways, railway-stations, mills, or other establishments likely to interfere with study. It is best also that the school-house be placed back some distance from the street, that the noise of passing vehicles may not distract or divert the attention of those engaged in study.

4. Beauty.—The beauty of the location, though often receiving but little attention from school officers, is one that should have its due influence in the selection of a site. Beautiful surroundings have much to do in creating a love for the beautiful. A school-house so situated that the children are brought face to face with the beautiful in Nature, and surrounded on all sides with such scenery as must necessarily make them love the beautiful from the very association, will have its beneficial effects not only on the discipline and order of the school, but also in the formation of the moral character of the pupils. Children coming from such a school can not fail to have a more refined taste and a purer moral character than those schooled amid surroundings which lack every essential element of beauty. The teaching of the beauty surrounding us is unconscious, but the lessons learned are none the less pleasing and none the less valuable. Every mountain-slope, every verdant valley, every winding stream, every charming landscape, has its in

fluence in forming character. Let children, then, always be surrounded with the beautiful, that the life within may be made to grow beautiful in harmony with the life without.

2. The Size and Proportions.—The size of a school building should of course depend on the number of pupils to be accommodated. In general, at least ten square feet of floor-surface should be allotted to each pupil, but fifteen square feet would be better. Thus, a school-room twenty feet by twenty-four might be made to accommodate from thirty-two to forty-eight pupils; one of twenty-four feet by thirty, from forty-eight to seventy-two pupils. The ceiling should be from ten to fourteen feet in height, according to the size of the room. A room twenty feet by twenty-four, and ten feet high, would give to forty pupils each one hundred and twenty cubic feet of air-space, while one twenty-four feet by thirty, and twelve feet high, would allow each of sixty pupils one hundred and forty-four cubic feet of air-space. A ceiling more than fourteen feet in height is a disadvantage rather than otherwise, as it makes a room more difficult to heat, with no special advantage gained in any other direction.

The proportions here indicated—twenty feet by twenty-four, twenty-four feet by thirty, and thirty feet by thirty-six—are among the best, the width being to the length in the proportion of about five to six.

When more than fifty pupils are to be accommodated, a recitation-room should be attached for the use of an assistant teacher.

3. The Architecture.—In the erection of a school-

2

house utility, beauty, and comfort must be combined. It is not more important that the school-house have a beautiful location than that it be beautiful itself and in harmony with its surroundings. Too little attention has been given to our school architecture as regards both beauty and comfort.

Neither beauty nor comfort necessarily makes the school-house more expensive. Comfort and fitness in the plan and construction should be the first considerations, but in connection with these beauty also should be taken into account, and both the form and the color be made to harmonize with the surroundings.

Plans.—A definite plan should be decided upon for the school-house before the proper officers begin its erection. This plan can in general be best prepared by an architect or some other person who has made the subject a study. When once the plan is fully adapted to the wants of the school, care should be taken that no changes are made by the builders. The fee paid to the architect for preparing the plan for a suitable building will be money well expended.

Cost.—The additional cost in adapting the plan of a building to the surrounding landscape is a matter of small moment when we consider the attachment which almost every child has for the school-house in which he received his early training. The beneficial effect exerted in both a moral and an æsthetic sense is of vastly greater importance than the few extra dollars expended in making the school-house a pleasant and attractive place and a source of pride to the community.

4. Internal Arrangements.—Closets.—Provision should

be made in every school-house for the storage of lunch-baskets, hats, shawls, etc. during school hours. Commodious closets or special cloak-rooms—one for the boys and another for the girls—should be provided, wherein these articles may be kept. These rooms or closets should always open into the school-room, that the teacher may have the pupils in sight, and thus prevent scuffling and unnecessary noise. These rooms ought to be about six feet by eight or six feet by ten, with shelves for baskets and hooks for hats and clothing. They may consist of a tier of boxes about ten inches square, instead of shelves. Each space and each hook should be numbered, and each pupil should have a number to correspond.

Library and Apparatus Space.—If possible, a room should be provided for the school library and apparatus. Shelves or closets at least should be put in convenient places, where the school library may be kept, the apparatus be stored, and a cabinet of minerals, grains, grasses, etc. be arranged for use. Without such provision the apparatus is likely to be neglected and become damaged, and the specimens in the cabinet scattered and lost.

Platform.—The platform may extend across the end of the room, though a platform half as long as the width of the room usually is sufficiently large. In height it ought to be not less than eight inches nor more than fifteen.

Space for the Blackboard.—Unless slate is preferred, it is usually quite as well to prepare the wall-surface at the ends of the room in what is known as "hard finish" by the use of calcined plaster or cement, that it may afterward be covered with a coat of liquid slating or a mixture of alcohol, shellac varnish, and lampblack. This space should be about five feet in height, and extend to within two feet of the floor. A trough should be placed below each board to catch the dust, and below this trough should be placed hooks on which to hang pointers and rubbers.

Arrangement of Seats.—Sufficient space for recitation-benches should be reserved between the platform and the first row of seats. The aisles between the rows of desks should be sufficiently wide to allow the pupils to pass back and forth readily without disturbing those occupied in study at the desks. A small aisle should be left in the rear of the back row of seats for the convenience of both teacher and pupils. The desks should be arranged so as to face the platform, and those for the smaller pupils should be placed nearest the teacher, leaving the larger pupils to occupy the rear of the room.

Flues.—These are needed both for ventilation and for carrying off the smoke and the gas generated by the heating apparatus. They should be so placed in the school-room as not to mar the beauty of the room, and yet effectually introduce pure air and carry off the impure as rapidly as possible. The ventilating flue and the smoke flue should be placed side by side, with a thin partition between, that the foul air may thus be heated and carried off through the chimney.

II. Arrangement and Size of the Grounds.

The chief points to be considered in connection with school-grounds are the following:

1. Size.
2. Convenience of Arrangement.
3. Beauty.
4. Appurtenances.

1. Size of the Grounds.—In cities, where land is high-priced, it is rarely the case that pupils have sufficient ground for either play or exercise, but in the rural districts, where the cost of land is not so great, certainly no excuse can be urged for being penurious in the matter of providing a sufficiently large playground. No schoolhouse should have less than half an acre of ground attached, but it would be much better if twice or three times this quantity could be allotted, particularly where there are several grades or several schools in the same building.

2. Convenience of Arrangement. — The play-ground should be so arranged that each sex may have a private play-ground in the rear of the house, where each shall be free from the intrusion of the other sex. The play-ground in front of the house should be common territory, where all may enjoy themselves under the eye of the teacher. The school building should be so placed that the larger portion of the school-grounds may be to the rear of the house. The ground should be well drained also, that it may be as dry as possible at all times, and the walks should be so arranged as to lead from the entrance of the grounds to each of the doors.

3. Beauty of the Grounds.—Not only may the school-ground be used for exercise and play; some effort should be made to render it beautiful also by adorning it with shrubbery, trees, and flowers. In planting trees

they should usually be arranged in groups, not in rows. The same may be said of shrubbery. Nothing shows a lack of taste more than the arrangement of shrubbery in lines along the paths and walks. As to the flower-beds, much may be left to the taste of the teacher and his pupils. Any good horticultural newspaper or magazine or floral catalogue will give more explicit directions than it is possible to give here.

The teacher should call in the aid of his pupils in ornamenting his school-grounds. He will thus not only cultivate their love for the beautiful, but also gain such a hold on their better nature as to make his discipline comparatively easy. Every pupil should be made to feel that he has an interest in preserving the beauty of the school-grounds, and that he has a right at all times to protect the shrubbery, the flowers, and other objects of beauty from injury.

4. Appurtenances.—Every school-ground should of course be supplied with the necessary out-buildings. In addition to these, certain pieces of apparatus designed to promote the physical education of the pupils should be furnished. Among the most prominent of these are horizontal bars, ball-alleys, swings, croquet sets, lawn tennis, and footballs. As to bats, balls, jumping-ropes, and hoops, the pupils will furnish these for themselves. A set of bows and arrows with targets, to be used in a private part of the grounds where all danger of hurt by accident may be avoided, would also prove of great benefit. All these will tend to make the school attractive to children, while they at the same time will do much to promote the physical welfare of the pupils. A few rustic seats placed where those not engaged in play

may become interested observers will add much to the attractiveness of the play-grounds.

III. School Furniture and Apparatus.

Each school-house should be fully supplied with all the furniture necessary to make the school a pleasant place and the teaching effective.

1. Desks.—The desks should be provided to accommodate not more than two pupils each, and in form they should be so adapted to the shape of the body as to make them as comfortable as possible. Hard-wood desks are preferable to home-made pine desks, and they are also much cheaper when service is considered. The desks should be graded in height and proportions to accommodate the pupils of different sizes. The seats in connection with the desks should be stationary. Loose chairs for pupils' seats are not well adapted to school work. Several chairs should be provided for the accommodation of visitors; also a suitable desk and a chair for the teacher.

2. Blackboard.—This is one of the articles of school furniture absolutely essential to good teaching and proper management. A blackboard is necessary in the teaching of every branch, and frequently it may be made a great aid in management by having some of the pupils, particularly the smaller ones, employ a portion of their time in drawing on it while others are busy in recitation.

Size.—The blackboard should not be less than four and a half feet high, and it should extend so low that even the smallest pupils may be enabled to use it. In length it should occupy at least one end of the room, but twice this quantity of board-surface is not too great.

How Made.—At present but little difficulty is experienced in securing good blackboard surface. Liquid slating is the best material. This may be placed directly on a smooth wall or board. Slated paper also may be used. Where the plastering is too soft for other surface the slated paper is particularly useful. Even good heavy hardware paper, or muslin put smooth on the wall, may be covered with slating or with a coat of paint having sufficient grit, and thus a good surface be secured.

Color.—As to color, there is room for choice, but green seems least tiresome to the eye. A good surface can be made by applying two or three coats of a mixture composed of shellac, turpentine, and lampblack, with just sufficient alcohol added to dissolve the shellac and enough lampblack to give good color. This black surface should then be covered with one or two coats of green liquid slating. It will make an excellent and a pleasing surface.

3. Erasers.—If possible, a sufficient number of erasers should be furnished to allow one to each pupil at the board. These erasers may be made of bits of sheepskin, of blocks covered with brussels carpet, or of heavy felt inserted in blocks similar to the Climax Rubber. Good erasers, such as will clean the board without throwing dust, should be used.

4. Pointers.—A number of soft-wood pointers should form part of the furniture. When teachers and pupils are required to furnish their own pointers they are likely to use any stick convenient at the time, and possibly injure the board-surface or the polish on the maps. Soft-wood pointers with smooth ends are the best, because they are less likely to injure the surface of either blackboards or maps.

5. **Reading-Charts.**—A set of reading-charts for the purpose of teaching primary reading should constitute a part of the school furniture. These need not be elaborate or expensive, but simply such as will add variety and interest to the textbook matter.

6. **Numeral Frame.**—No primary or ungraded school should be without a numeral frame. Not only counting, but also all the fundamental rules, may be taught concretely by the aid of this important little piece of furniture.

The chief remaining apparatus for illustrating *mathematical* work are the following:

A set of **Weights and Measures**, to familiarize the pupils with the practical part of Denominate Numbers.

A set of **Metric Weights and Measures**, to illustrate the Metric System and compare its various units with the system now in use.

A set of **Geometric Forms**, including cubes, cubical blocks, cones, cylinders, spheres, prisms, etc.

7. **Geographical Apparatus.**—For the purpose of teaching geography properly *Outline Maps*, *Globes*, and *Geographical Boards* seem to be the most important.

Outline Maps are necessary for teaching the contour and comparative size of the various countries, as well as for teaching local geography. A State, and, if possible, a county, map should form part of every set. Maps should remain open as much as possible, that pupils may become familiar with the outlines of countries, location of capes, etc. by their constant presence.

A **Globe** is necessary in teaching the shape of the

earth, its motions, and the comparative size, as well as the location, of countries, etc. on its surface.

A Geographical Board, with a rim around the edge, and containing on its surface sand, clay, water, and rocks, may be used to illustrate the natural divisions of land and water. A board of two or three feet square is sufficiently large. Pupils with a board of this kind will spend many a pleasant hour in illustrating geographical facts.

8. Cabinets.—These can probably be best secured by the teacher. Pupils, when they find the teacher interested, will gladly assist in collecting minerals, plants, leaves, grains, grasses, and other botanical, geological, or zoölogical specimens for the purpose of making a cabinet. The interest which may be awakened on the part of pupils, and the culture of the observing powers thus secured, are of the greatest importance.

9. Dictionary.—An unabridged Dictionary is one of the important articles of school apparatus. The smaller dictionaries are so limited in their definitions, and so unsatisfactory, that they answer only partially the end for which they are intended. It is best, therefore, to have an unabridged, or at least what is known as a comprehensive, dictionary for school use.

How to Secure Apparatus.—It is unquestionably the duty of Directors or School Trustees to provide from the public funds all the necessary furniture and apparatus for each school. In few instances, however, is it likely these officers will furnish all the apparatus here mentioned. In the event of their failure in this respect, how may it be secured?

1. A Demand should be Created.—The judicious teacher by proper effort may do much toward awakening not only his school, but also the community, to the necessity of having a better supply of apparatus. He can do this partly by showing what may be done with simple apparatus of his own construction. An address to the citizens of the district, showing how much better the work of teaching may be done with apparatus than without, will do much to convince his patrons.

2. By Entertainments.—An entertainment given by the school children will usually secure the attendance of both parents and friends; and when it is known that the proceeds are to be devoted to the purchase of apparatus, the patrons will attend all the more willingly. This entertainment may consist of a contest in Spelling, Geography, History, or some other branch of study, or it may consist of readings, declamations, music, etc., judiciously intermingled. Now and then also a lecturer may be secured who is willing to deliver an address for the benefit of the apparatus fund.

3. By Subscription.—Another plan for securing funds for the purchase of apparatus is by subscription. Let the subscription-list be headed by a few of the most liberal citizens. This, accompanied by a personal appeal to every citizen of the district, will rarely fail in securing an amount sufficient to form the nucleus of a collection of apparatus, or in adding to that already in possession of the school.

IV. School Hygiene.

Nothing in connection with school management can be of greater importance than the preservation of the

health of both teacher and pupils. Not only a knowledge of the laws for preserving health, but also a strict
compliance with these laws, is necessary. School hygiene
has special reference to the following in connection with
the school-house and the pupils:

1. **Lighting.**
2. **Heating.**
3. **Ventilation.**
4. **Condition of Floor and Walls.**
5. **Posture.**
6. **Exercise.**
7. **Play.**
8. **Hygienic Habits of Pupils.**

1. Lighting.—Light is an essential to health. Dark
rooms are never so healthful as those properly lighted.
Well-lighted rooms are also more pleasant and inviting
than those from which the light is to any great extent
excluded. Many diseases of the eye with which they
who work in-doors are often afflicted might be avoided
if the laws for the preservation of sight were properly
understood and observed.

The Windows of every school building should be high,
rather than broad and low. The nearer to the ceiling
the light enters the room, the more nearly will Nature be
imitated in giving us sunlight from above. The windows should also be placed only on the sides of the room,
and never in such a position that the light will strike
either the teachers or the pupils in the face.

Curtains and Shutters should not be used for the purpose of shutting out the light or the sunshine, but
rather for modifying it and preventing injury to the eyes

by its glare. When curtains are placed at school-room windows, care should be taken that they be made of such material as will intercept as little of the light as possible.

Books with Small Type should, as far as possible, be avoided. One of the evils with which we have to contend in this age of cheap books is the small type in which so many are printed. Narrow pages and good-sized type with ample light would do much to preserve the eyesight of our children.

2. **Heating.**—The temperature of the school-room should be such that every occupant is comfortably warm whatever part of the room he may occupy. With a stove in the centre of the room this is almost impossible. No more defective plan of heating a school-room could be devised than this. The great difficulty, as every intelligent teacher knows, is that while those in the immediate vicinity of this central stove are frequently too warm, those sitting nearer the walls are too cold; and thus, in either case, the foundation for disease is laid.

Steam-heating is not only the most comfortable, but also probably the most healthful, for the reason that the air is not scorched and robbed of its oxygen by this method. For a large school building with a number of departments or rooms it is also economical. In small school buildings the expense of steam apparatus would be proportionately too great.

An Open Fireplace is one of the most healthful and pleasant ways of heating where wood is plentiful, and the draft created is also beneficial in connection with the proper ventilation of the room.

Ventilating Stoves, constructed on the plan of the open fireplace, are equally effective. Either plan requires a large and constant supply of fresh air; and thus, while the room is kept warm, the air is also comparatively pure.

Hot-air Furnaces may be used in the heating of school-houses where steam-heating is found to be too expensive. The furnaces should be located in the cellar, and the radiating surface be constantly supplied with a current of fresh air from without. Running side by side with the heat flues should be ventilating flues, to carry off the impure air of the room; and these should be open at or near the floor, that the carbonic acid gas floating near the bottom of the room may be drawn in, heated, and carried up the flue. The serious objection to hot-air furnaces is, that the air becomes parched and too dry, thus often causing very serious diseases of the throat.

Stoves in most cases, particularly in rural districts, are the usual means by which the rooms are heated. If possible, these should be placed in the cellar in the same manner as the hot-air furnace; but if this is not possible, they should be placed near the side or the end of the room, and should be encased with sheet iron or some similar material, so as to distribute the heat gradually. Two small stoves in opposite corners of the room prove much more effective than one large one placed either in the centre or at the side of the room. If the stove be encased, a flue conveying fresh air from the outside and along under the floor may be made to open directly under the stove, thus supplying not only heated air, but also pure air.

3. Ventilation.—Good school work needs pure blood, and pure blood needs pure air. The wonder is, not that we do so little in our schools, but rather that we do so much in an atmosphere so deficient in the essential elements of animal life, and so loaded with poisons and effluvia. School-houses must be well ventilated in order to have pupils do good work. A few hints only can be given here on methods of ventilation.

Heat Flues.—Under these may be included open fireplaces, ventilating stoves, and similar contrivances, by which the lower stratum of air in the room is drawn directly into the fire and made to pass up the chimney. In this last may be included also the ventilating flue built in connection with the smoke flue, as previously suggested. The separating partition between these flues should be of sheet iron, so that sufficient heat may pass through to rarefy the impure air and carry it out at the top of the building.

Window Ventilation.—When not overcrowded, schoolrooms may be effectually ventilated by placing a close-fitting board of five or six inches in width under the lower sash of each window. In this manner a flue is made by the overlapping of the upper and the lower sash, and a constant stream of fresh air is admitted, which comes in at such a part of the room as to become heated before reaching the occupants. This plan may be used in even the severest weather.

Outside Flues.—The plan of securing fresh air by the use of an outside flue is similar in principle to the method of window ventilation advised. The outside flue is simply a box-flue or pipe open at the lower end, and communicating at the upper end with the school-room at a point near the ceiling. The heated air of the room will not escape through this pipe, because it will not descend; cold fresh air will flow through the tube into the room, and, meeting the warm air of the room, will also become heated. No possible draft can be created. This outside flue may be from six to ten feet or more in length, and may run up by the side of the window-frame, or it may be so built in the wall as not to mar the beauty of the building. A wire screen should be placed over the outside opening, so as to prevent leaves, etc. from entering.

Pipe Ventilators.—These consist of ventilating pipes running close by the side of the stovepipe, and opening within a few inches of the floor close by the stove. The air in the pipe becomes heated, a draft is created, the impure air near the floor is drawn into the ventilating pipe and carried near to the point where the stovepipe enters the chimney; here the ventilating pipe enters the stovepipe, and the impure air joins the smoke in its ascent to the chimney-top.

Door Ventilation.—In school-houses consisting of several rooms the omission of carpet-strips under the doors serves a good purpose in permitting the heavy impure air to flow out. Opening the door for a few seconds occasionally will do much toward purifying the air in the school-room. In no case, however, should the door be left open long enough to make any one uncomfortable. It is better to open the door frequently for a moment at a time than open it for a longer time but at greater intervals.

During pleasant weather both windows and doors may be left open much of the time. When the room is ventilated in mild weather, it is best to raise the lower sash and lower the upper at the same time, that the danger of drafts may as much as possible be obviated.

Reflectors.—Where the top of the window-frame is square a reflector may be attached in such a way as to throw the air toward the ceiling as it enters. The only objection to this plan is that the reflector will to some extent interfere with the light.

4. Condition of the Floor and Walls.—So far as cleanliness concerns the school-room, it has to do mostly with the condition of the floor, the walls, and the desks.

The Floor.—There seems to be no good reason why the floor of the school-room should not be kept as clean as that of one's own home, yet few school-room floors receive a thorough cleansing more than once a term. No good housewife would permit forty or fifty little folks to run over her kitchen floor six hours a day for a single week without insisting upon giving that floor a thorough cleansing; and yet we permit these same children to occupy the school-room in a similar manner for sometimes three months or more, and are satisfied with a single sweeping a day. Mud from the shoes, excretions from the body, dust from the streets, and other filth are permitted to accumulate on the floor, only to be stirred up by each moving class, thrown into the air, and breathed into the lungs of both teacher and pupils.

The bits of paper, nut-shells, apple-parings, etc. which so often vex and worry the teacher are not half so detrimental to health nor half so objectionable as this filth which is permitted to accumulate from day to day.

The Walls.—What has been said of the floor is equally

true of the walls of the school-room. In many cases the
dust is allowed to accumulate during a whole term, and
in some cases for a much greater length of time. Here,
too, the germs of disease may accumulate, only to be dis-
seminated as the breezes of spring and summer are permitted to enter the room and disturb them. To say
nothing of the lack of neatness, this filth may in time
become the source of sickness. A good teacher will see
to it that the walls of the school-room are kept clean.

The Desks also should be kept as free from dust as
possible. Too often the sweeping is done in such a
manner as simply to shift a large part of the dust from
the floor to the walls and the school furniture, where it
is allowed to remain. Pupils should be trained to take
pride in the condition of their desks and the surrounding furniture. A word of commendation now and then
to those deserving it for keeping their desks neat and in
good order will do much toward securing both clean furniture and good discipline.

5. Posture of Pupils.—Whether sitting or standing,
the posture of the pupil should be one of ease and
grace. In general a graceful posture is easy, and an
easy one is graceful and healthful. An erect posture,
with the chest well forward and the shoulders back, is
the most conducive to health. Under all circumstances
sitting in a stooping posture over the desk should be
avoided. In this position the chest becomes contracted
and the lungs cramped, so that they are incapable of per-
forming their work of purifying the blood, and the body
thus becomes enfeebled and diseased.

Comfortable Seats, of such a height that the feet of the

children may rest comfortably and firmly on the floor, are necessary. The backs of these seats should be curved, so as to adapt themselves to the shape of the body and give support at all points. The seats should also be a little higher in front than at the rear, in order to support the legs and prevent slipping forward.

The Height of the Desks should be made to conform to the varying heights of the different pupils. With desks too high incalculable damage may be done to the child in causing such a curvature of the spine as to raise one shoulder higher than the other, and thus produce a lifelong deformity. Low desks are equally objectionable, because the pupil is apt to lean forward and assume an injurious stooping posture.

6. **Exercise.**—Exercise is necessary to health. Without exercise the body becomes enfeebled and sickly, the various physical organs perform their functions imper fectly, the vital forces are diminished, and at last disease lays hold on the organization and death ends the career of the child.

Exercise is necessary to study. A sound mind needs a sound body. The mind is to a great extent influenced by the bodily health. A weak or enfeebled body is rarely accompanied by a strong mind. But exercise is necessary to strength and soundness of body, and therefore necessary to strength and soundness of mind.

Calisthenic Exercises.—For in-door exercises probably nothing is of more value than calisthenics, with or without music, but music should accompany the exercise whenever possible. For beginners these exercises should be very simple, and of such a character that all the children can readily follow the lead of the teacher. For older pupils they may be more complicated.

The value of these exercises is very great. They can be called into use at any time to wake up the school. The movements, all being made in exact time, train to promptness, while they also develop grace of body and motion. They are interesting, and therefore they may be made to take the place of play. They promote harmony of action, and thus train pupils to act in concert in the performance of other duties.

Gymnastic Exercises also are useful in promoting health. These may be regulated, as in the case of a march or a drill, or they may be unregulated, allowing each to follow the inclination of his own will. In either case they will prove of much benefit to the pupils if conducted in such a way as to call into play as many muscles of the body as possible.

The Place for Exercising.—As to the proper place for exercising, little need be said. All exercise should be taken in the open air when possible. When the weather is such that exercise must be taken in-doors, calisthenics or light gymnastics may be used, but pure air should be admitted freely through the open windows while the exercise continues, unless the cold be too severe.

7. Play.—Play may be regarded as the most healthful of all exercise. It is the natural exercise for children. They cannot help playing. No other form of exercise can be profitably substituted for it. Richter says: "Play is, in the first place, the working off at once of the overflow of both mental and physical powers." The play is in the child, and it serves the valuable purpose of exercise and recreation at once, while it strengthens and develops the physical powers and keeps them healthy. To the student play is what quiet and rest are to one wearied by the performance of manual labor.

The Place for Play.—In pleasant weather all plays should be carried on in the open air. This not only because there is more room, but because it is much more healthful. Wherever possible the school-house should have a dry cellar or a basement story, where pupils may enjoy their sport when the weather prevents their playing out of doors. Should such a place not be provided, the next best arrangement is to allow pupils to play in the school-room, but in every such case the teacher should select the play. The play should be such as will not cause the furniture to be injured or raise the dust from the floor. A pleasant in-door play, in which both boys and girls may engage, is that of tossing bags of beans or corn from one to another. These bags should be made to contain about a quart. There is no possible danger of doing any harm to the furniture or the walls should they happen to strike either.

The Time for Play.—The proper times for play are usually the recesses or intermissions. How many recesses a day the pupils should have, and how long these periods should continue, must be left somewhat to the judgment of the individual teacher. Two recesses each half day, with at least an hour's intermission at noon, is not too much play-time for the smaller pupils. For the older pupils probably one recess each half day in addition to the noon intermission would be sufficient. Now and then a half or a whole holiday, with a short excursion or a picnic, would be of great benefit The tendency among all classes of schools, the Kindergarten excepted, is to do too much work and have too little recreation, and the result is most unsatisfactory.

Character of the Play.—The faithful teacher will give some attention to his pupils while on the play-ground as well as when in the school-room. The boys will naturally choose the rougher plays, while the tendency among the girls will be to select those of a more quiet character. Both extremes should be avoided. Any plays among boys in which they are likely to do one another personal injury, or plays which will train them to become rude and rough, should be prohibited; and, on the other hand, girls should be encouraged to engage in those plays which will give them physical vigor and endurance. The teacher who advises his girls not to engage in such plays as will give them healthful physical development, and who cautions them continually to be dignified and observe the laws of decorum instead, commits a crime for which his ignorance is no excuse.

The Teacher's Influence in Play.—If the teacher be wise in his supervision of the children's sports, he will exert a powerful influence in the formation of character. A kind word of praise now and then will cause each participant in the play to put forth extra exertions in order to win the approbation of the teacher; and the teacher, on the other hand, will find his discipline a much less difficult matter if his pupils feel that they really have his sympathy in their plays.

Should the Teacher engage in Play?—Why not? If his joining in the play will help to make it interesting, there seems to be no good reason why he should not help his pupils in their sports. The p'ay-ground is an excellent place for the study of character. Of course the teacher should not permit himself to be drawn into any disputes with his pupils. Under no circumstances should he forget that when off the play-ground he is the teacher and his playmates the pupils. If, however, the teacher have not perfect control of his pupils in the school-room, it would likely be unwise for him to make himself one of the participants in a game where evil-disposed pupils might be inclined to degrade him or take revenge. Should the teacher engage in play, it would not be wise for him to reprove or punish while on the play-ground. His example should be such as to command the highest respect of his pupils. Should anything improper occur, the reproof had better be administered privately after the excitement of the game is forgotten.

8. **Hygienic Habits of Pupils.**—Attention must be given to the personal habits of pupils. Much of the impurity of atmosphere in our school-rooms is caused by improper ventilation, but much arises also from the lack of personal cleanliness on the part of our school children. Some of this negligence is due to ignorance of hygienic laws, and much of it to the carelessness of both parents and children. The special hygienic features to which attention must be given are—

1. Cleanliness of Person.
2. Cleanliness of Clothing.
3. Correction of Offensive Personal Habits.
4. Supply of Food.
5. Abundance of Sleep.
6. Cheerfulness of Disposition.

1. Cleanliness of Person.—A washbowl and a number of towels are among the essentials of school-room equipments. The teacher should see to it that his pupils have their teeth carefully brushed, their hair neatly combed, and their hands and faces washed clean before they begin the day's work. Not only this: he should insist that the hands and faces be kept clean and the hair kept neatly combed. If he could induce the children to have their shoes and boots polished also, himself setting the example, he would be doing a good work. But more than this: he should explain to them the importance of bathing frequently, not only during the summer, but also during the winter. Soap and water are friends to civilization, and few men appreciate so fully the necessity for the use of both as does the teacher of a district school. Pupils should be taught that bathing is necessary to health and physical vigor, and they should be advised to cleanse the skin frequently also as a preventive of disease.

2. Cleanliness of Clothing.—But little less important is the cleanliness of one's clothing. A frequent change of underclothing should be advised, that the excretions of the body may not be carried around for a week or more. Pupils should also be requested to come to school with their clothing brushed. They should be made to understand that all wraps, shawls, comforters, scarfs, etc. should be put aside when in the school-room, that they may serve the proper purpose when worn out of doors.

3. Correction of Offensive Personal Habits.—Care should be taken by the teacher to correct improper and offensive personal habits on the part of his pupils. Spitting on the floor or the stove should be condemned publicly, and it would be in place to suggest that no one ought to

be without a pocket-handkerchief, nor ought he fail to use it when necessary. Offensiveness to one's associates demands this, to say nothing of personal cleanliness. Picking the teeth in company or in class ought to be rebuked, at least in private, and any other personal habits that offend should receive similar treatment.

4. **The Supply of Food.**—The teacher can do little here except to recommend a proper diet. Food of proper qual ity should be supplied and in sufficient quantity, but with this the teacher has nothing to do. He can, however, advise his pupils as to the hygiene of eating so far as thorough mastication or too rapid eating is concerned. He ought also to break up the bad school habit of lunching at every recess, showing pupils the necessity of taking meals at regular times.

5. **Abundance of Sleep.**—Sound sleep and plenty of it is essential to hard study. Sleep is the time for repair. The teacher should impress on the minds of his pupils the importance of regularity of habit in the matter of sleep. Seven or eight hours is not too long a period of sleep for those who perform active mental labor, but the hour of retiring and of rising should be as nearly as possible the same all the year round. It is not the " early to bed and early to rise " so much as it is the regularity which " makes man healthy, wealthy, and wise."

6. **Cheerfulness of Disposition.**—Cheerfulness is conducive to health. The cheerful teacher's presence is worth more than the most learned and logical doctrines of the man who relies on his grimness and dignity to control his school. Of all places in the world, home and school should be made the most cheerful. The teacher who is cheerful will have a school of cheerful

and animated pupils, and more good, honest hard work will be done in a school of this kind in a month than could be done in one of an opposite character in a year.

A cheerless teacher should never be permitted to associate with small children. The teacher whose august presence frightens his pupils, and who controls them by fear, is out of place in a school-room; and no Board of Directors should give employment to a person of such a temperament. Youth is the sunshine of life, and no clouds should be permitted to cast their shadows over the happiness which God has implanted in the glad young hearts of children.

Suggestions on School Hygiene.

1. Diplomas should not be secured at the expense of health. It is better that our boys and girls should grow up healthy men and women than that they should acquire scholarship at the expense of physical prostration and bodily deformity.

2. See that all your pupils exercise, and that the exercise be pleasant.

3. Regulate the plays of your pupils in such a way as to make them most beneficial physically and mentally.

4. Assign no lesson for home study to children under ten years of age.

5. Suggest pleasant reading to your pupils as a mental recreation.

6. Do not encourage precocious children by rapid promotion or over-praise; rather hold them in check.

7. When children are sick do not permit them to study.

8. See that your school-room is well ventilated, but be

careful that children are not subjected to unnecessary drafts of air.

9. Give frequent talks to your pupils on hygiene in such language as they can readily understand.

10. Explain to your pupils how to preserve their teeth.

11. Show them the importance of wearing their clothing loose rather than tight, and explain why the former is more healthful.

12. Explain to them the importance of thorough mastication of their food.

13. Explain to them the necessity of bathing frequently and taking plenty of sleep.

14. Show them the importance of retiring and rising at fixed hours.

15. Tell them what articles of diet are wholesome, and what otherwise.

16. Show them that they can prevent sickness by observing the laws of health.

17. Have them assume such positions, whether sitting or standing, as will permit the lungs to expand fully.

18. Impress upon them frequently the importance of taking good care of their bodies and preserving the health, even at the expense of great knowledge.

19. Do not permit your pupils to hold their books in such a way as to cause near-sightedness.

20. Recommend to them proper hygienic reading—such books as will teach them to know themselves and preserve their physical vigor undiminished.

V. School Grades.

A system of graded schools divides pupils according to their attainments into several divisions, each of which is accommodated in a separate room.   Thus the more advanced pupils are made to constitute a grammar school or a high school, while the beginners would properly be known as a primary school.

Advantages.—The chief advantages of graded schools are the following:

1. They Save Labor.
2. They are more Economical.
3. They are Productive of Better Teaching.
4. They are more Easily Governed.
5. They Prompt the Ambition of Pupils.
6. They Furnish Education in the Higher Branches.

1. **Graded Schools Save Labor.**—In a well-graded school the number of classes is much smaller than in one ungraded.   The experienced teacher discovers also that a class of twelve or fifteen pupils is more interesting and more readily taught than if the same pupils were distributed in two or more classes.   A large class requires no more time to teach than one having a smaller number of pupils, and by this combination of classes much labor is economized.

2. **They are more Economical.**—Since graded schools require a smaller number of classes, the number of teachers is diminished, and thus a saving in the cost of teaching is effected.   Graded schools also save expense in the purchase of apparatus and in the building of school-houses, particularly in villages and larger towns.

3. **They are Productive of Better Teaching.**—The number of classes being reduced, the teacher in charge has more time for the special preparation of the various

lessons to be taught. The number of branches taught in the different departments of a graded school is smaller than that of a mixed school; and here also time is saved, and the teacher is enabled to prepare himself better for his work. It is true also that a teacher who limits himself to the teaching of a few branches will do much better work, especially if these are to his taste, than if he attempt to teach all the studies of a school course.

4. They are more Easily Governed.—In a graded school the pupils are usually nearly of the same age; there are, therefore, fewer causes for disturbance than would naturally exist in a school where pupils of all ages associate and recite in the same room. The easiest school to govern is usually that in which the children are most nearly equal in age and attainments. In a graded school the fear that they may, as the result of improper behavior, negligence, or idleness, fall behind their classmates, is a strong incentive to keep pupils obedient and orderly.

5. They Prompt the Ambition of Pupils.—Not only does the fear of falling behind their classmates tend to good order among pupils in a graded school, but there is also a desire created to excel and prepare for promotion to higher grades. Every pupil, having in his mind this promotion from one grade to another, will strive more earnestly to succeed and keep pace with his companions in their efforts to reach higher departments.

6. They Furnish Education in the Higher Branches.— Graded schools are not meant to take the place of academies, colleges, or other higher institutions of learning; but, inasmuch as many of the brightest children are so situated pecuniarily that it is impossible for them to

attend any higl. school under private control, the graded
school properly supplies a demand which exists in every
district.   Talent is not the possession of one class of
society alone; and since it is to the advantage of the
state to develop all talent to its fullest extent, certainly
the graded school, because it offers opportunities for
higher education which could not be secured through
any other means, ought to receive the encouragement
of every one interested in the education of the whole
people.

Objection to Graded Schools.—The chief objection
urged against graded schools is that they suppress individuality.   All the pupils being made to conform to a
certain line of study, it is urged that individual talent
must necessarily be neglected, and that this tendency to
uniformity will thus suppress the efforts of genius to
make itself felt.   If the objection be sound so far as it
applies to graded schools, it must be regarded as sound
in its application to all schools that do not give special
attention to the development of special talents.   But
public schools do not aim at making specialists.   The
best they can do is to give the rudiments of a general
education, leaving special education to technical schools
which prepare for special callings.

The Number of Grades.—The number of grades is in
a great measure governed by the number of pupils.
Where the number of pupils is less than one hundred
but two grades could be established.   From one hundred to one hundred and fifty pupils would require
three grades, and above that number at least four grades.

In some cities the division is into Primary, Secondary, Grammar, and High Schools. Others divide into Primary, Secondary, Intermediate, Grammar, and High Schools. By this latter arrangement two years may be given to each of the divisions except the High School, which ought to have a course of study covering three or four years, thus making the school life eleven or twelve years in length.

By subdividing each of these divisions into classes A and B there is constant annual promotion from class to class from the time the child enters the schools until he quits them. Thus at the end of the first year, if his work has been satisfactory, he may be promoted from the B class Primary to the A class Primary; at the end of the second year he goes from the Primary to the Secondary, and so on until he reaches the High School, where, if he be diligent and studious, he ought to be promoted from class to class until he has completed the whole course of study. Thus there is a constant incentive urging him forward from the beginning to the close of his school life.

The number of grades must be determined partly also by the course of study to be pursued, a fuller course requiring usually a greater number of grades. It will be found that the number of pupils in the primary grades will be much greater than that in any other, and there will be a gradual decrease in number up to the High School.

Manner of Grading.—The two chief methods of grading are the Union and the Separate Graded Schools.

The Union Graded Schools usually have all the pupils

in one building, with a principal or a Superintendent, who has charge of all the schools, but with an assistant for each room. A modification of this plan, where the number of pupils is sufficiently great, consists in having a General Superintendent, with a principal for each department, Primary, Secondary, etc. This plan requires an assembly-room for each department, with recitation-rooms attached.

The Separate Graded System locates the various grades in different parts of the district, the Primary School by itself, the Grammar School by itself, and so on. In this case also a separate principal may be provided for each building, with a General Superintendent for the whole town or city. The lower grades under this system should be located at the most convenient points, while the higher grades should be placed near the centre of the district, particularly if this be also the centre of population.

Graded Schools for Country Districts should be formed wherever the number of school children is sufficiently large to furnish the material for two or more grades. Many country districts might have a central Grammar or High School, if so inclined, by placing the school-houses for the primary pupils at the most convenient points, and locating the Grammar School near the centre of the district, or where it would prove most convenient of access to the greatest number. If, then, the admissions to this school were made on merit alone, as shown during the term and at examination of the primary schools of the district, a powerful incentive to study would be given to all the pupils of the district.

The Kindergarten.—The Kindergarten—literally, a " children's garden "—is a primary school intended for children too young to enter upon the ordinary school work. The Kindergarten system was first used by an eminent German teacher, Friedrich Froebel, who had been one of Pestalozzi's pupils.

The leading feature of Froebel's system was that of directing the active play-principle of childhood into useful channels. Children were brought together and surrounded with such conditions that their own free actions would lead them to the best self-development. The teacher acted chiefly as a guide. Plays were so arranged that each in its turn became instrumental in furnishing the child new ideas and in developing new activities.

The methods of the Kindergarten are mainly the wise direction of play. The kind of play is selected by the child, but the method is controlled by the teacher, and is so directed as to convey some important lesson. Singing constitutes one of the main features of Kindergarten work. The pupil finds his work pleasurable, and thought is developed because the teacher tells little, and allows the child under careful guidance to discover truth for himself.

VI. School Aids.

A well-regulated school needs, in addition to the apparatus heretofore mentioned, certain general aids designed to promote study and good order. These are—

1. Textbooks.
2. The School Library.
3. School Records.

1. Textbooks.—Textbooks are a necessity in the work of teaching. Oral instruction and lectures have their proper place in a school course, but they cannot be substituted for the textbook. The mind is disciplined bv study, and the requisite study can be secured only in connection with a properly-arranged book. Next to a live, energetic, and interesting teacher, the textbook is the most important educational agency for giving to the child the proper mental discipline. The discipline afforded by the difficulties which the child overcomes in his study of a good textbook is of vastly more importance than the recitation or any possible course of oral instruction. But it must never be forgotten that no textbook can cover all of the ground, and that it is therefore the duty to supplement and add to the instruction conveyed by the book.

The Objects of Textbooks.—1. They give Reliable Information.—The knowledge given by a good textbook is not only put in such a shape as to make it at once available to the learner, but it is also reliable, and the information conveyed is stated in more concise language than it would be if imparted wholly by oral instruction. This is of great advantage to both teacher and pupil, as it leads to clearness of thought.

2. They Secure System.—Under purely oral instruction the language of the teacher as he states and restates his principles must necessarily lead to looseness of thought on the part of his pupils. This is particularly true in the case of younger pupils. Clearness of statement and logical arrangement of parts in a textbook will tend to make pupils systematic. Indeed, a well-arranged text-

book is a great aid to students in systematizing their methods of thought and work.

3. They Employ the Time of Pupils.—In all kinds of schools there must necessarily be much time in which the pupil is not engaged in recitation. The textbook utilizes this by giving the pupil an opportunity to keep himself busy and at the same time gain mental discipline by systematic study.

4. They Aid the Teacher.—Few teachers indeed are thoroughly competent to communicate the knowledge claimed at their hands, or communicate it in so intelli gent a manner, as does the textbook, which aids the teacher by presenting facts in a concise and systematic way, relieves him of the necessity of making special preparation to put his knowledge in logical shape, and saves much time which would be required to separate the essential from the non-essential parts.

The Characteristics of Good Textbooks.—The characteristics of a good textbook are as follows:

1. It should be Logically Arranged.—A properly-arranged textbook is not only a great aid to the pupils in pursuing a study, but it is also an important help to the teacher in conducting the recitation. The principles and facts stated should not be fragmentary. Each, so far as possible, should be connected with knowledge previously acquired or statements previously presented. A logically-arranged textbook induces logical modes of thought, and thus in itself furnishes valuable discipline.

2. A Textbook should be Clear.—The language of a textbook should 'be so clear that the learner cannot misunderstand it. In the statement of principles or prob-

lems the pupils should not be left in doubt as to the meaning by any ambiguous construction which a sentence may bear. Facts should be stated in such clear language that the learner may apprehend the meaning at a glance. Textbooks of this character tend to simplify greatly the work of both teaching and learning.

3. A Textbook should be Interesting.—Textbooks may be made interesting by their arrangement as well as by the matter they are made to contain. They ought not to be a mere mass of dry facts; the principles enunciated should be illustrated by such examples as will attract the attention of the learner, and at the same time elucidate the subject treated in such a way as to make him comprehend. The most important principles and the most interesting facts should be given, and these in such a way as to lead the pupil to love study.

4. The Textbook should be Brief.—A textbook is not designed to present an exhaustive discussion of any subject, and it ought not, therefore, to be made too comprehensive. A suggestive textbook that leads the pupil to original investigation or the consulting of cyclopædias and dictionaries is much more valuable than one which attempts to be exhaustive in its treatment. True, a book may present all the most important facts and principles of a branch of knowledge and be a good textbook, but the best books always leave much for the teacher to add or for the learner to find out for himself.

5. The Style of a Textbook should be a Model.—The style in which a textbook is written should not only be clear and the language such as the pupil can readily comprehend, but the thoughts should be presented in such a forcible and yet graceful way as to attract the

attention. It is too often the case that an author's style is so labored or his language so obscure that the student finds great difficulty in deciphering the meaning. The language should be not only choice, but also correct. Nothing will have a stronger tendency to throw doubt on the statement of an author than the fact that he does not use his own language correctly.

6. **The Textbook must be Adapted to the Capacity of the Student.**—In general, they can write textbooks best who best understand the operations of the child-mind, and they understand child-mind the best who constantly associate with children, and who, as teachers, observe the mode of thought which the child follows. A book written in such style or such language as is beyond the capacity of the child to grasp is not only useless, but it also is pernicious. In such case the child will either commit the words of the book to memory without understanding what is meant, or become discouraged and lose interest in the study. All textbooks, therefore, should be adapted to the capacity of the class of pupils for whom they are intended, and this both in style and language, as well as in the matter presented.

7. **A Textbook should be Attractive in Appearance.**— The chief requisites to a beautiful textbook are good paper, attractive illustrations, and good-sized, clear type. It is a serious mistake to use broad pages and small type for any textbook. No one can estimate the injury done to eyesight by textbooks of this character. When the page exceeds three or three and a quarter inches in width it tires the eye more or less in passing from one line to another, and the broader the page the greater the injury. The cost of manufacturing books with good type and good

paper is but little greater, comparatively, than that of manufacturing those of poorer material. The same rule of economy that is good elsewhere is good here —that good goods, though higher in price, are the least expensive.

The Abuse of Textbooks.—No greater educational fallacy has been presented than that which urges teachers to do away with the textbook. The ultimate result is found to be a breaking up of habits of study and a destruction of mental discipline. The only compensating result is a mass of fragmentary knowledge which hardly deserves the name. Even did teachers know everything in connection with the subjects they teach, textbooks would be a necessity in order that pupils might discipline their minds by study. But, under the present condition of things, to urge teachers to throw aside the textbook and attempt to impart all instruction orally is worse than absurd; it is criminal. The difficulty lies not in the too frequent use of textbooks, but in their abuse. The following evils may be named as the most important in the use of the textbook :

1. **Committing the Text to Memory.**—There are certain portions of every textbook which must be committed, but one of the chief abuses of the textbook consists in committing everything verbatim, and attempting to recite in the exact language of the book. Definitions and principles stated in exact terms by the author cannot likely be improved upon by the student, and it is better, therefore, that such of these as are important be committed. But in the relation of incidents or the statement of facts the pupil ought to be permitted to use his own language

when it is correct. It is not the book, but the subjects, which he studies and which he ought to recite.

2. The Teacher's Use of a Single Textbook, with no knowledge beyond, is to be condemned. The teacher who goes before his class with no knowledge of anything outside of the textbook used in school is not well fitted for his position. He may be able to deceive his pupils if he be well versed in the textbook used, but the knowledge he imparts will be of little consequence, and the enthusiasm which a teacher ought to arouse among his pupils will in his case be found wanting.

3. The Teacher should Supplement the Textbook.—It is not enough that he teach only what is found in the book, or that he take upon himself the duty of simply asking questions on the text or as found on the printed page. This ought to form but a small part of the recitation. The teacher ought to encourage his pupils to read other books on the subjects he teaches and observe for themselves. But, above all, he ought to inform himself thoroughly on the subject-matter of the textbook by consulting similar works, and give his pupils the benefit of his reading, while he at the same time stimulates the pupils to greater effort. He should make the textbook matter the text or groundwork on which to base additional instruction.

The Selection of Textbooks.—This important duty is left to the respective School Boards. The teacher, however, should be consulted, and wherever possible his recommendation should be the guide for the Board's action. This, too, for the reason that the teacher understands best the wants of both himself and the pupils,

and knows best what style of book would render teaching most effective. Merit of course should be the gov-·
erning principle which should decide for or against the
adoption. Changes in textbooks should not be made
frequently, but when worthless books are in use, and
better ones can be had at but little additional expense,
no false notion of economy or fear of narrow public
sentiment should for a moment deter a Board from
doing its duty in adopting the best books.

The Ownership of Textbooks.—By far the most economical plan in the securing of textbooks is that of
having them purchased and owned by the school district. Pupils and patrons purchase at retail rates, but
School Boards could make satisfactory arrangements
with publishers to secure textbooks at much less expense.
These books could be paid for out of the school funds of
the district. They should be charged to each pupil when
distributed, and credited to the same pupils at the end
of the term if returned in good condition. Payment
should be required for those damaged or lost. It would
be wise for the legislatures of the various States to enact
laws which would empower the various School Boards
thus to make school textbooks, as well as pencils, chalk,
and other school equipments, the property of the district.

2. **The School Library.**—1. Its Importance.—Next to
the school itself, one of the most important educational
agencies in a community is the school library. But
comparatively few books find their way to the table of
the rural citizen. Nothing will so soon supply this
want as the establishment of a library in the public

school to which all, but particularly the children of the district, may have access. The taste for reading created in the child while at school will grow, and in the end we shall have as the result broader culture and a higher grade of citizenship. The study of textbooks alone. while it will discipline the mind, will not give this broader culture It needs the reading of the best thoughts of our great authors on literature, science, and art.

2. **The Books to be Chosen First** are those which will enable the pupils to gain knowledge outside of the textbook. These will embrace—first, a dictionary, if one be not included among the apparatus supplied by the Board; also cyclopædias and other works of reference. To the cyclopædias should be added historical works, treating not only of the United States, but also of England, France, Germany, Greece, Rome, etc. Then should follow the works of the most prominent British and American poets, and with these the prose-writings of Irving, Prescott, Dickens, Thackeray, Scott, Hawthorne, Cooper, Macaulay, Carlyle, Holland, and others. A taste could thus be created for the elegant in both prose and poetry, while the vitiated taste created by the cheap, flashy literature of the day might be anticipated and supplanted.

3. **How to Secure the Library.**—The same suggestions might be made here that were made with reference to securing apparatus. The chief methods to be recommended are entertainments and a subscription fund. An appeal to the School Board by the teacher and a committee of prominent citizens would have great weight. An appeal to the citizens to make donations

of books to the library might be effective. First of all, however, an interest in establishing a library should be aroused and a demand for reading created. Much could be done in this matter by an energetic teacher's making direct personal appeals to his patrons. The library once established, the School Board should vote a small sum annually for the purchase of new books and the rebinding of old ones.

4. The Management of the Library. — During the school term the management of the library should be placed in the hands of the teacher. Books of reference should of course be consulted in the room, and in no case ought they to be carried to the pupils' homes. The teacher should kindly consult with his pupils in the selection of books, adapting the reading as far as possible to the taste of the individual minds. The pupils should be required to handle the books with care and return them in good condition. The books of reference should be placed where they can be consulted at any time, but all other books should be given out at a specified time, as Friday afternoon of each week. During vacation it would be well to place the library in the care of some citizen, who might keep the school-room open on alternate Saturdays or on every Saturday for an hour. It is quite as important that the library be used in vacation as during the school term, that the taste once acquired for reading may not be lost.

3. School Records.—Among the aids to school management school records play an important part. The chief forms which these records may take will be determined by the attendance, the deportment, and the class-

recitation, thus giving three forms of records. This number may, however, be reduced to two, the first containing a record of admission and attendance, and the second a record of deportment and class-recitation. A form for these registers need not be given here, as blank forms are in many cases supplied by the State, and others may be had at but small expense from publishing-houses.

The *chief advantages* of school records are as follows:

1. **They are an Incentive to the Teacher.**—The fact that here is a daily record of the attendance and deportment of each pupil, which may be compared with that of other schools in the district, induces the teacher to put forth special efforts to secure regular attendance and proper deportment on the part of his pupils. The records enable him also to systematize his work and keep in mind more steadily the standing of his pupils. With these records the possibility of his doing injustice to the pupils is also in a great measure avoided.

2. **They are an Incentive to the Pupil.**—The child who feels that every absent-mark is recorded against him for the inspection of any who may desire to consult the record, and that his conduct and progress are registered also for inspection and future reference, will not fail to put forth his best efforts to please the teacher, unless, indeed, he be lost to all sense of shame. Every experienced teacher knows with what eagerness he is approached by even young men and young women desirous of knowing their class-standing at the close of an examination or at the end of a school term. A private note sent home at the close of the week or the current month, giving the absent-marks and the class-standing of a negligent pupil, will often have a good effect, not only

on the child, but also on the parents. The reading aloud of the general average of each pupil, when judiciously done, may also occasionally have a good effect.

3. They Furnish Information to Patrons.—One of the chief uses of school records is to furnish information to the patrons and the school officers, and thus enable them to judge of the comparative progress and attendance of the respective pupils. They also enable the school officers to compare the relative standing of the individual schools in a district, and judge of the comparative standing of the same school from year to year.

4. They Furnish Information to the New Teacher.—But few schools are fortunate enough to have the same teacher in charge for any great number of consecutive years. New teachers taking charge without the aid of school records and registers are compelled to work blindly for a time. But where these records are well kept and handed down from each teacher to his successor, the incoming teacher is enabled to begin his work intelligently and avoid loss of time.

The following are the chief *objections* urged against the use of class records:

1. They Require too much Attention.—This objection is not urged against the attendance roll, but chiefly against the class record showing the daily progress or class-standing. In small schools the objection is not valid, but certainly in large schools, if pupils are marked at each recitation, considerable valuable time will be consumed in this way. Postponing the marking until the close of the school for the day does not seem to be a good plan, for the reason that it is almost impos-

sible to remember distinctly the merit of each pupil's individual recitations for the day.

2. The Judgment of Teachers Differs.—It is urged that what would be considered a meritorious recitation by one teacher would in the estimation of another more rigid be deemed only passable, and thus the marks would so vary as to lose all value. It is urged also that a teacher is likely to mark differently according to his moods and the condition of his health—that when in a pleasant mood the marks will be higher than when he is despondent or suffering from ill-health, consequently the register would not record accurately the progress of the pupils.

There is some force in each of these objections, but the advantages of school records so largely outweigh the disadvantages that we think they ought to be used. Of course they must be judiciously kept and the teacher must be conscientious in his marking. If properly used they will prove a valuable aid in school management. ·

CHAPTER II.

School Organization.

School Organization consists in such a systematizing of the school employments as will enable the teacher and the pupils to do the greatest amount of effective work with the least friction and in the shortest possible time. A complete organization is one of the essentials to success. If the work of the school be systematized, and all school appliances and school machinery be so arranged as to do the work most efficiently, the difficulties in discipline will be reduced to a minimum and the labor of learning will become a pleasure. The work of organizing an ungraded school is a difficult task, even for an experienced teacher, and in the hands of a beginner the task becomes doubly difficult. To provide for the efficient education of the child mentally, morally, and physically, is a work requiring not only much careful thought, but also great skill and patience.

The First Day of School is one of the most important in the term. It is necessary to make a good beginning and create a favorable impression on the pupils the first time the teacher meets them. The trial is a serious one, but it need not be feared if the teacher has made all the necessary preparation to make a good impression and win the pupils to him. Nor will the influence he wields be limited to his pupils; these in turn will communicate their opinion of the teacher to the parents, and judgment will be promptly rendered.

The Teacher should Visit the Neighborhood before the opening of school. This he may do a week or two in advance or a few days in advance, but in either case he should meet some of the most prominent Directors and citizens, whose acquaintance he should cultivate and whose advice and friendship he should strive to secure before beginning his responsible work.

The Views of the Community with reference to school work should be among the first things to claim his attention. It will be a matter of prime importance for him to know whether the citizens of the district are progressive or otherwise, that his plans may be adapted to their educational wants in such a manner as to cause the least friction. These facts he can best learn from the intelligent citizens, while at the same time he is enabled to pave the way for securing their co-operation in his work.

A second object of the visit is that of *learning the methods of management and teaching pursued by the previous teacher.* This can be best effected by consulting the previous teacher personally if he reside in the neighborhood, and if not, then by consulting some of the most intelligent school officers or citizens of the community. Having once learned these methods, he should be careful not to criticise them or speak disparagingly of his predecessor's work, but rather make such changes as he may deem necessary in a quiet, unostentatious way.

A third object of the visit is that of ascertaining *what changes may be necessary or prudent,* either in the management of the school or in the methods of instruction. Previous to making such changes it would be wise for the teacher to submit them to the school officers and influential citizens with the view of securing their indorsement and support.

Suggestions.

Be Early at School.—If possible, the teacher should be at the school-house and have everything ready for the day's work before the pupils arrive. A few kind and cheering words of welcome to each pupil as he comes will do much to win for the teacher the friendship of the children and make the first day's work successful.

Have your Plan of Work Ready.—No time should be lost in wondering what to do first. The teacher should have his plan of organization prepared, and make use of it at once. As soon as the pupils have become seated a few pleasant remarks may be made, showing that the teacher is desirous of making the school pleasant and profitable to the children and the community, and asking kindly their help. The better nature of the children may be reached in this way, and the cases are rare in which the teacher will not find his efforts sustained by both pupils and parents.

Assign Work Promptly.—The classification of your predecessor, even though defective, will be sufficiently accurate for the first half day's work. Have your programme arranged, so that classes may be called upon without delay. Quite a good plan is that of assigning lessons to the reading classes first, and when these are called upon to recite, other work may be given to them which they can prepare after returning to their seats. All may thus be kept busy, and this in itself will be conducive to good order.

Be Cheerful and Patient.—Nothing will tend to secure ready obedience on the part of the pupils so much as the cheerfulness and patience of the teacher during the first day's work. Do not become nervous and attempt to accomplish too much. It is not possible to make the machinery work as smoothly the first day as when the school is fully organized, and it is folly for any teacher to worry and fret because he thinks he is not accomplishing enough.

Seating.—In the choice of seats for the first day it is best for the teacher not to interfere, unless some of the smaller pupils should attempt to occupy the desks properly belonging to the larger ones. In that case a quiet request will likely be all that is necessary to secure the required change. It may be well to announce that the pupils will be permitted to retain such seats as they have chosen, so long as the occupants do not interfere with the good order of the school, but that the teacher reserves the right to make a change whenever the welfare of the school makes it necessary.

Temporary Signals may be devised for the convenience of both pupils and teacher. Thus, for the purpose of asking permission to leave the seat or ask a question the pupil may raise the hand and receive the assent of the teacher. Some excellent teachers pursue the plan of having a special signal for each request, as the raising of one finger for permission to speak with a neighboring pupil, two for permission to come to the teacher's desk, three for permission to leave the room, and so on.

Temporary Rules.—The teacher must not make the mistake of drawing up a series of rules for the government of his pupils the first day of school. Indeed, the

best management is that which will postpone all necessity for these rules indefinitely. Not until the conduct
of the pupils becomes such as to justify the rules should
there be any mention made of them. One of the most
serious mistakes of inexperienced teachers is that of de-
pending upon a list of inflexible rules by which to govern a school.

Permanent Organization.

No school organization can be regarded as strictly
permanent. No teacher can foresee all the difficulties
with which he will have to contend, and in the nature
of things it will therefore be impossible for him to
anticipate them by any perfect scheme of organization.
The best he can do is to watch carefully the working of
his temporary organization, and adopt such features of
it as may seem to him worthy of being preserved permanently. He will need, however, to add such other
features as may seem to him necessary to secure profitable and effective work. Among these will be proper
classification, a well-arranged programme, effective school
signals, and proper attention to the manner of opening
and closing school, the seating of pupils, and the recesses.

1. School Classification.

School Classification consists in grouping pupils in
classes according to capacity or advancement for the
purpose of study and recitation. Close classification
puts each pupil in the same class in all studies, and
gives him an opportunity of equal advancement in all
branches. Loose classification permits the pupil to

recite his studies in different classes according to the advancement he has made.

In the lower-grade schools the plan of close classification is much the better. Should pupils find themselves in advance of their classmates in some branches and not equal to them in others, there is all the more reason why they should devote less time to those studies in which they are most proficient and more to those about which they know least.

In the higher-grade schools it is often convenient to adopt the plan of loose classification, particularly in the case of such pupils as may have neglected the study of some of the necessary branches while they were in the lower grades, also in the case of such pupils as may have but a short time to attend school, and are desirous of giving special attention to a few studies only.

Advantages of Classification.—The following may be named as the chief advantages of classification:

1. Classification Enables the Teacher to Estimate the Comparative Progress of his Pupils.—In no way can the teacher judge of the actual work of his pupils so accurately as when they meet in class-recitation, where all have the same work to perform.

2. Classification Makes Teaching more Effective.—An explanation may be made as readily to a whole class as to a few individuals. The teacher is thus enabled also to make special preparation for each recitation—something which would be almost an impossibility in a poorly-classified school or one wholly unclassified.

3. Classification Economizes the Time of both Teacher and Pupils.—Particularly is this true in the case of the teacher. An illustration or an explanation given to a class is equivalent to the same illustration or explanation given fifteen or twenty times to as many individual pupils. The recitation of a whole class need not consume much more time than the recitation of a single pupil, particularly if all the members are attentive.

4. **Classification Stimulates Pupils.**—Children will work more diligently if they have classmates. The competition of classmates is an incentive to exertion. The presence and the criticism of classmates also have a beneficial effect in making the pupils anxious to recite well and make proper progress in study.

5. **Classification Makes Enthusiastic Teaching.**—Small classes are usually most easily governed, but larger classes give a teacher inspiration and arouse enthusiasm; and this enthusiasm is in turn almost sure to make teaching successful.

6. **Classification Cultivates Attention.**—Pupils reciting in groups or classes find an incentive to closer attention in the fact that their work is likely to be criticised. They become attentive also, because they are desirous of criticising the errors of others; and, in general, the desire to surpass their fellows will assist in leading them to give close attention to the preparation as well as to the recitation of the lesson.

Principles of Classification.

Certain principles govern the classification of pupils in all kinds of schools. Among these are—

1. **Age and Scholarship.**—These are the chief criteria for determining the class which a pupil should enter. In general, scholarship ought to have most weight in determining the classification, but it is often best to put

an older pupil who is backward in scholarship with those near his own age, even though they are in advance of him, that he may not be discouraged. Older pupils sometimes feel keenly the embarrassment of being classed with those much younger than themselves, and whenever it is possible such classification should be avoided.

2. **Advancement.**—Care should be taken to adapt the classification to the advancement of the pupil. If classed too low, he is apt to become careless and indolent; if too high, he may be discouraged in finding himself unable to keep pace with his classmates. Strong, healthy pupils may, as a general thing, be classed higher than the more delicate, because capable of harder work and greater endurance.

3. **Average Ability.**—Care should be taken to classify according to the average ability of the child. Pupils are rarely found to be equally advanced in all branches. Some who are well advanced in arithmetic are deficient in language, while others well advanced in language or geography will be found deficient in mathematics. The average ability in all these branches should be the basis of classification. It is always best to have pupils give close attention to those studies in which they are most deficient, that the culture they receive may be as symmetrical as possible.

4. **The Standard of Classification.**—No definite rule can be given as to what branches-should be made the standard of classification. Reading is an unsafe standard, for the reason that those who have had the advantage of good libraries, children's magazines, and newspapers at home, and who have read much silently, will

be found much better readers than those not enjoying these advantages, though probably not any farther advanced in the usual school studies than others of their own age.   Arithmetic is probably the safest branch on which to base classification, for the reason that deficiency in any other branch may be remedied, but deficiency or backwardness in arithmetic is difficult to overcome, and it often greatly interferes with the pupil's progress in other studies.

5. The Number of Classes.—The number of classes in graded schools will be governed by the closeness of the grading and the number of grades. Usually, two classes, or at most three, will be found sufficient. In ungraded schools the number of classes ought not to exceed five, and in many schools the number might profitably be limited to four. This of course supposes that all the members of a class pursue the various studies of that class, unless for some important reason they be excused. Those in the lower classes will have fewer studies than those more advanced, so that there will not be the maximum number of classes in each branch of study.

6. The Size of the Classes.—The size of the classes also will be determined somewhat by the size of the school. Medium-sized classes in public schools are best. Where it is possible classes should contain from ten to twenty pupils each. In primary studies a smaller class is not objectionable, as the attention of the younger children is more liable to wander, and with them the larger the class the more difficult the task of holding the attention. The class should never be so large that but a portion can recite each day. If possible, every pupil should be reached during every recitation.

Suggestions.

The following suggestions will be found useful in class-ifying pupils:

1. **Adopt the Classification of your Predecessor as a Temporary Classification.**—This will furnish the basis to build upon, and you will avoid criticism and difficulties in the beginning.

2. **Let it be Known that your First Classification is Temporary.**—Pupils will then be less dissatisfied when removed from one class to another.

3. **Do not Classify too High.**—One of the mistakes of ambitious students and misguided parents is that of de-siring to advance too rapidly. Pupils belonging properly in the Third or the Fourth Reader should not be pro-moted to the Fifth until they are fully prepared. This interferes with progress, and gives the pupil a mere smat-tering of knowledge.

4. **Avoid Conflicts with both Pupils and Parents.**—Rather let pupils be classified too high at first than awaken the op-position of both themselves and their parents. The pupils will see their mistake in the daily recitation, and usually they will be found willing after a short time to take their proper places.

5. **When Making the Permanent Classification, Let it be on Merit.**—If parents or pupils object, explain to them and convince them of their mistake.

6. **Do not Compel Pupils to Pursue Studies to which their Parents Object.**—It is true you have the right to enforce such compulsion, but it is neither wise nor necessary to do so unless the omission of such study interferes ma-terially with the progress of the pupil in other branches.

The wise plan is to remove the difficulty by convincing the parent of his error.

7. **Do not Give too many Studies.**—The tendency among pupils is to undertake the study of more branches than they can pursue profitably. The teacher should so construct his programme as to avoid this, and permit the pupils to study only as many branches as they can study well. More than this will defeat the end of study.

8. **Let the Studies be such as will Give Variety.**—This will secure symmetrical culture and keep up interest. The pupil will also be able to do more work with less fatigue, just as the exercise of all the muscles will cause less fatigue than the continued exercise of a single set.

2. Programme.

Among the essentials of good school mangement is a a well-arranged programme. To make provision for all the classes, assigning to each its proper place and fixing for each its proper limit of time in recitation, is a work of some difficulty. A good programme should have the following *characteristics :*

1. **A Definite Period** must be fixed for each class-recitation, for every intermission, for all interruptions, and for study. All these must have their place, that the school work may be well done.

2. **The Length of the Recitations** must be arranged according to the size of the school and the number of classes. The shortest time should be given to the smaller pupils, and the longest to those more advanced.

3. **The Frequency of Recitations** must be provided for. The primary pupils will need several recitations a day in most of the branches, in order to keep them interested as

well as busy, while the more advanced pupils will need but a single recitation in each branch. Some of the higher branches may even have recitations on alternate days, but it will be found difficult to keep up a proper degree of interest where the recitations are not heard daily.

4. **All Studies should Have their Proportionate Share of Attention.**—Neither arithmetic nor any other hobby of teacher should be permitted to occupy a fourth or a third of the time, leaving the remainder to be divided among a half dozen other studies.

5. **All Grades of Pupils must be Provided for.**—The smaller as well as the larger must receive due attention in class-recitation, and a just proportion of time should be allotted to each in the programme.

6. **Studies to be Prepared in School should not be Recited among the First.**—In general it will be found most convenient to prepare all mathematical work in school. Classes in arithmetic should not, therefore, be among the first to recite in the morning. The first recitations of the day should be either the lessons prepared at home in the evening or the classes in reading.

7. **The School-day should not Close with severe Mental Labor.**—Classes in penmanship, drawing, spelling, or vocal music should end the day's work. Class exercises needing steady nerves, such as writing or drawing, ought not to follow a recess or any time of physical exertion.

8. **The Programme must Provide a Time for General Business.**—The teacher will frequently have remarks to make to the school, reproof may need to be administered, or cautions may need to be given. None of these ought

to interfere with the recitations of the day. A special time, therefore, for this general business should be provided in the programme.

9. **The Programme should Provide for all the School Work.**—Let it be remembered that recesses are for rest and recreation. Neither the pupils nor the teacher should be employed in work at that time. Both need the recess. Nor should recitations be heard after school. To detain pupils beyond the regular school hours for the recitation of lessons is both cruel and unwise.

Advantages of a Good Programme.

The chief advantages of a well-arranged programme are the following:

1. **It Leads to Regular Habits of Study.**—Study becomes systematized, and students learn to do their work according to a plan.

2. **It Makes Systematic Teachers.**—A fixed plan will make the teacher systematic in his work, and the duties of the school will be performed with less friction and greater regularity.

3. **It Saves Time.**—No time is wasted in attempting to recite half-prepared lessons. The pupils, knowing the time when they will be expected to recite, are prepared and ready.

4. **It Makes Systematic Pupils.**—It not only leads to regular habits of study, but it makes pupils regular and systematic also in all their other work and in their habits of life.

5. **It is an Aid to Systematic Organization.**—Each new teacher is enabled by the programme of his predecessor to take up the work just where it was left at the close

of the preceding term, and carry it on without embarrassment or loss of time.

6. **It Makes School Work Effective.**—No time is lost. Pupils know not only when they will recite, but also when lessons may be prepared to the best advantage. The development is harmonious, and all jarring and discord of conflicting classes are avoided.

In all cases when a new programme is to be used, it is best to post it in some conspicuous place where the pupils may consult it.

Probably no programme can be arranged to suit all classes of schools, but the two following are offered as a basis on which to work. The first is designed for a school of four classes, and the second for a school of five. Either may be modified to suit the requirements of the school in which it is used. In the following model for a programme the first column denotes the time for the opening and the close of each recitation; the second, the class which is to recite; and the third, the branch of study in which the recitation is to be conducted:

PROGRAMME.

FORENOON.			AFTERNOON.		
9.00	...	Opening Exercises............	1.00	...	Roll-Call, etc.
9.10	D	Reading and Spelling	1.05	D	Reading and Spelling.
9 20	C	Primary Geography............	1.15	C	Arithmetic.
9.35	B	Primary Geography............	1.30	B	Arithmetic.
9.50	A	History or Geography.......	1.50	A	Arithmetic.
10.10	D	Language Lessons	2.15	...	Writing and Drawing.
10 25	...	Recess...	2 35	...	Recess.
10 40	C	Language Lessons............	2.50	D	Object-Lessons or Reading.
10.55	B	Language Lessons............	3.00	C	Reading and Spelling.
11.25	A	Grammar	3 15	B	Reading and Spelling.
11.50	D	Numbers..................	3 35	A	Reading and Spelling.
12.00	...	Noon Recess	3.55	...	General Exercises.
			4.00	...	Dismission.

PROGRAMME FOR FIVE CLASSES.

	E	D	C	B	A
9.00– 9.05..	Op'ng	Exercises.			
9.05– 9.15..	Reading.	Reading.			
9.15– 9.25..	....	.. ..			
9.25– 9.40..	....	....	Geography.	Geography.	History or Geography.
9.40–10.00..	....	Recess.			
10.00–10.25..					
10.25–10.40..	Language Lessons.	Language Lessons.	Language Lessons.	Language Lessons.	
10.40–10.50..	....	....	......	....	
10.50–11.05..	....	....			Grammar.
11.05–11.20..	....	....			....
11.20–11.45..					
11.45–12.00..	Numbers.	Numbers.			
1.00– 1.10..	Reading.	Reading.			
1.10– 1.20..	....	....			
1.20– 1.35..			Arithmetic.	Arithmetic.	Arithmetic.
1.35– 1.55..			....	....	....
1.55– 2.15..	Writing,	...e School.			
2.15– 2.30..		Recess.			
2.30– 2.45..	....	....			
2.45– 2.50..	Spelling.	Spelling.			
2.50– 3.00..	....	....	Spelling.		
3.00– 3.10..	....	....	Reading.	Reading and Spelling.	Reading or Spelling.
3.10– 3.25..	....		.	....	
3.25– 3.40..	....				
3.40– 4.00..	....				

3. School Signals.

A system of school signals, if not too complex or cumbersome, will tend to systematize the school work and save much time. It will also be productive of good order and tend to make pupils methodical.

The following *principles* should govern a code of signals:

1. **The Signals should be Few in Number.**—The tendency is to use too many signals, and the result is confusion. Many teachers themselves make their school noisy by the too frequent use of the bell or by having too complicated a system of signals. But few signals, and only those which are readily understood, should be adopted.

2. **Each Signal should be Necessitated by the School Work.**—All arbitrary signals, or those used only for display, should be avoided.

3. **Each Signal should be Significant.**—Every signal should have its definite meaning, and should be used for the same movement or request, without variation.

4. **Promptness in Obeying Signals is Important.**—Unless pupils be trained to obey each signal promptly, the system is useless. The movements should also be made quietly as well as promptly.

5. **The Signals should be Well Understood.**—Pupils should know definitely what is required of them, and they should in time become so well acquainted with the code that they act almost automatically in response to any signal made.

The following simple code of signals will be found useful:

I. In Calling School.

In calling school, either in the morning or after any of the recesses, two signals only are necessary:

1. The ringing of a bell to call pupils in;

2. A tap of the bell or a word to call them to order preparatory to beginning work.

II. In Calling Classes.

In calling classes to recite three signals are sufficient:

1. The teacher's voice or a tap of the bell calling for attention;

2. A tap of the bell for the class to rise;

3. A tap of the bell for pupils to pass to the recitation-seats.

III. In Dismissing Classes.

In dismissing classes but two signals are needed:

1. A tap of the bell for pupils to rise and face their desks;

2. A tap of the bell for the pupils to pass to their seats, or, if the class be not too large, it may be dismissed without any signal whatever.

IV. In Dismissing School.

In dismissing school four signals may be used:

1. "Attention!" called by the teacher;

2. A tap of the bell for the pupils to arrange desks;

3. A tap of the bell for the pupils to rise;

4. A tap of the bell for the pupils to march out by sections.

If no means of having your pupils march to music be at hand, either the teacher or one of the pupils may count one, two—one, two, to ordinary march-time, and dismiss the children in this way. The pupils will enjoy the march.

4. Hand Signals.

Special signals may be used by pupils when desirous of speaking to the teacher or to one another ; also when desirous of asking or answering questions in class.

The chief class-signal is that of raising the hand—either, 1. To express a willingness to answer ; 2. To criticise or correct ; or, 3. To ask a question.

When a pupil is reciting no one should be permitted to attract attention or confuse him by raising the hand, and particularly the snapping of fingers should never be tolerated. Many a pupil has been thoroughly confused by the ill manners or the thoughtlessness of a classmate who raised his hand or snapped his fingers while the former was reciting.

Each pupil should be held responsible for every answer. Therefore, if a mistake is made all the pupils who noticed it should raise the hand when criticism is called for. As soon as the teacher designates one to make answer or criticise, the other hands should be dropped.

Frequently, pupils may have occasion to ask questions while at their seats. In such cases the pupil should raise his hand before speaking, and should remain quiet until the teacher recognizes the signal and permits him to speak. Only in extreme cases should the teacher permit any one to raise the hand while a class is on the floor reciting. While pupils are reciting the teacher's whole attention should be given to the recitation, and interruptions should be postponed until a change of classes takes place.

Suggestions.

1. Avoid calling your pupils to class without any system.

2. Avoid calling out your pupils to class one by one as you name the numbers—first, second, etc.

3. Avoid permitting your pupils to scramble in a disorderly way to the class for the purpose of securing a choice seat or a desirable position.

4. Avoid permitting your pupils to run to their seats or to class.

5. Avoid permitting your pupils to crowd one another.

5. The Opening and the Closing of the School.

The simplest and least showy plans of opening school are generally the best. The following plan has been well tested and found successful:

Singing.—After the pupils have assembled, the teacher, or, if he is not a good singer, one of the pupils, leads the school in an appropriate hymn or song, in which all join. This will cheer up the children and put them in a good humor for the day's work.

Scripture Reading.—In communities where no serious objections are raised the singing should be followed by the reading of a selection from the Bible, without note or comment. Should there be any pupils in the school whose parents object to having their children present when the Bible is being read, these should of course be excused.

Prayer.—Nothing seems more appropriate than that the Lord's Prayer, repeated in concert or chanted by the whole school, should form a part of the opening exercises.

Roll-Call.—Following the foregoing exercises should come roll-call. This need occupy but a short time. A convenient plan is that of having each pupil numbered, from one upward. When ready the teacher announces, *Roll!* and the pupils, beginning with the first, respond *one, two, three, four*, etc. The numbers failing to respond may be placed on the blackboard, where mistakes may be corrected. From this corrected list the teacher is enabled to record both his tardy pupils and his absentees.

Intelligence Class.—Immediately following roll-call the teacher may hold a short intelligence meeting of the whole school. In this exercise important items of news may be communicated by such of the pupils as may have gleaned any; and to these should be added such as the teacher may have gleaned since the preceding day. When news is scarce the reading of a short but interesting story will serve to attract the pupils and bring them to school in good time.

The Afternoon Session may be opened with singing, followed with roll-call, as at the morning session, but omitting the remaining portion of the morning exercises.

The Manner of Closing School is a matter of importance. The day's work having been finished, it is highly important that every one leave the school-room in the best of spirits. Let the teacher start a cheerful song, and have all his pupils join. Make the exercise such that every pupil may leave the school with the feeling that it is a pleasant place, and with a hearty wish to return on the morrow. At the close of the song a tap of the bell or the teacher's voice will call the pupils to attention, and

6

they may then be dismissed according to the signals heretofore suggested.

6. Seating.

1. **Sex in Seating.**—Discipline is sometimes secured by seating the two sexes in alternate rows or sections, but the inexperienced teacher will find the plan of placing the girls on one side of the room and the boys on the other much the safest and the least likely to cause him annoyance. The policy of seating boys and girls promiscuously at any time while engaged in school work, unless it be in recitation, is a doubtful one.

2. **The Right to Change Seats.**—The teacher should at all times reserve the right to re-seat pupils. When a pupil becomes talkative or troublesome to his neighbors, he should be removed at once to a separate seat if possible. Various reasons may exist why pupils should be removed from one seat to another, and the teacher alone has the right to make the change.

3. **Discipline by Seating.**—The teacher may often avoid difficulties in discipline by seating properly. As far as possible, one pupil only should be permitted to occupy a desk. Two talkative pupils should not be seated together. The weak should be placed with the strong. Troublesome pupils should be placed where they can cause the least annoyance. All seating should be so arranged as to secure the best possible order.

7. Recesses.

Times for recreation are quite as necessary in the school day as are times for labor. Long-continued work will accomplish less and tire more than work judiciously interspersed with play.

1 **The Number of Recesses.**—If possible, two short recesses of ten minutes each should be taken each half day. If this cannot be done, then one of at least fifteen minutes should be substituted, and all should be permitted to enjoy it. The teacher's discipline ought not to be so weak that he finds it necessary at any time to keep pupils in during the play-hour.

2. **The Teacher at Recess.**—The teacher needs the reereation afforded by recess quite as much as the pupils do. He should supervise the play of his pupils. It will cheer him up, and fit him to do the work of the schoolroom all the better because of the recreation.

3. **Pupils and Teachers should Associate at Recess.**—The teacher should associate with his pupils during recess, and join in pleasant conversation with them. He has no higher duty than that of making school pleasant to those placed in his care. His example as the companion and guide of his pupils should always be worthy of imitation. The wise teacher often exerts quite as powerful an influence on the play-ground as in the school-room.

4. **Interruption Recesses.**—Provision should be made for interruptions. There should be some fixed period, as the time for changing classes, when two minutes, or as much time as may be necessary, may be set apart for the purpose of allowing pupils to ask questions, receive permission to leave their seats, or take a short rest.

5. **Irregular Recesses.**—Now and then the teacher will find that with his most skillful efforts order cannot be preserved. Confusion seems to reign supreme. The very atmosphere seems to be saturated with anarchy and discord. Any effort to make the discipline more rigid seems only to make the confusion worse. Scolding and

whipping serve only to increase the restlessness and nervousness. What shall the teacher do? Let him give the pupils some recreation, some rest, and enough of it to overcome the effects of the disturbance. Occasionally stopping all the regular exercises and joining in a calisthenic drill or a cheerful song or two will be all that is necessary to bring every one under perfect control again. Sometimes a five-minute recess will secure the same result, and bring order out of confusion.

CHAPTER III.

School Work.

THE chief work of the school, so far as pupils are concerned, is study. Education is not a pouring-in process, in which the pupil is a mere passive receiver. The mind needs culture, and it receives its best culture through study. Many questions arise here: What are the objects of study? How may pupils be trained to study? How may habits of study be inculcated? What are proper incentives to study?

I. Study.

1. The Objects of Study.

The chief end of education is development in the fullest sense of the term—intellectual, moral, and physical. One man is better educated than another only so far as his powers are more fully developed and under better control.

The chief object of study is *Discipline* or *Training*. To this may be added the subordinate ends of study— *Knowledge, Expertness, Moral Culture, Aspiration.*

1. Discipline.—All man's powers, whether mental, moral, or physical, need culture and training in order that they may be strengthened and receive the highest possible development. Discipline is the true end of study. An undisciplined mind works at a disadvantage, and accomplishes but little. The knowledge gained

85

during one's school life is of much less importance than the systematic training which the mind acquires under the wise guidance of a teacher who understands the true end of education, and how best to train and develop the natural powers of both mind and body with which God has endowed the child.

Training to Think is the most important work that the teacher has to perform. Thinking must be systematic. The pupil must be made critical and observant; his attention must be undivided; his memory must be exact; his judgment must be clear. He must be trained to see quickly, exactly, and sharply. The branches taught must be used to give him self-discipline and self-development.

The Pupil must be Taught How to Study.—The chief work of the teacher is to guide and direct the pupil in his efforts. The efficient teacher never does the work of the pupils for them. Patient efforts must be made by the teacher to show his pupils how to study the various branches in a systematic way, so as to give the best culture to the mental powers. It is a serious mistake to permit pupils to pursue their studies in an unsystematic manner. Energy is thus wasted and time lost. An occasional hint even as to what part of a paragraph is important, and what may be omitted without disadvantage to the student, will prove valuable. But the teacher can do better than this by watching constantly, and directing the pupil how to pursue each study in such a way as to afford the best mental development.

2. **The Acquisition of Knowledge.**—This is also one of the objects of study. Knowledge is as essential to

the mind as is food to the process of physical growth, but it should never be made the chief end of study. The mind craves knowledge as the stomach craves food, but in either case the ultimate end is development. The physical organs assimilate the food, and it is made to supply the physical loss and strengthen the body. The mind assimilates knowledge, and the mental powers systematize it and adapt it to the wants of mental development.

The great error in teaching is, that the acquisition of facts and principles is the chief object of education. Even teachers sometimes make no distinction between knowledge and education. A man may have a great fund of knowledge, and yet be but indifferently educated. His knowledge may be of little avail to him, because of his lack of power to use or apply it. Education is not the mere process of communicating known facts. Knowledge is a means of education rather than an end.

3. **Expertness.**—Expertness is also an end of study. Knowledge which we cannot apply is of little value. The man who is unable to make his knowledge available has but little force in the community. The mind of the educated man is better disciplined, and therefore better able to do the world's work. The educated man is a power which makes itself felt, not only in business, but also in society. True education gives one that efficiency which makes him a leader in everything that tends to elevate his fellow-man.

A False Object.—The expertness spoken of here is not that efficiency which one acquires in preparing himself to accumulate wealth. This, it is true, is by many considered the prime object of all education. The ability to drive sharp bargains, to make money, etc., is to some extent acquired by intellectual training, but it should not be regarded as one of the objects of study. The object of education is not to assist one to escape from labor, but rather to make his labor skillful. An ignorant man works like a machine, without thought and without improvement, but educated labor is skilled labor, and therefore intelligent.

4. Moral Culture.—This is also an end of study. Fichte says: "The ultimate end of all education is to lead men and human society toward their highest moral destiny. Education must be based not on utilitarian considerations, but purely on the considerations of humanity." Character-building is one of the chief aims of all education, and therefore of study. The discipline which produces a well-balanced mind will have its due effect in giving proper moral culture.

5. Aspiration.—Study gives purer ideals. Nothing is more effective in awakening within the student those noble aspirations to a higher life than the examples of the great and the good with which he comes in contact in his daily study. He builds imaginary castles, it may be, but the work does him good, even though they do "vanish into thin air" before the rude breezes of a practical, every-day life. He sets for himself a high mark, and, even though he may be powerless to reach it, his efforts lift him above the plane he occupied before, and give him a broader view of life and his relation to the world. His contemplation of these ideals gives a charm to his life which ennobles him, and helps him to appreciate more fully his relations to God and humanity.

2. Conditions for Successful Study.

Effective study requires proper conditions and surroundings. The best work can be done only under the most favorable circumstances. These have been partially discussed in treating of School-Houses and School-Furniture. The following conditions also are important:

1. **Bodily Health and Comfort.**—It is not only necessary that the pupil have a sound body to insure a sound mind, but it is necessary also that he be comfortable during study-time. Pure air and correct hygienic habits are essential. The room should be comfortably heated and the light properly modulated. The stomach should be free alike from the gnawings of hunger and the oppressed feeling of too full a meal. The head should be clear and free from the effects of either a cold or a disordered stomach. The whole system should be as nearly in its normal condition as it is possible to put it, and the teacher should see that the child is as comfortable as may be.

2. **Favorable Surroundings.**—It is necessary that the surroundings of the pupil be such as to induce study. The room should be pleasant and quiet should be preserved. The old-time method of mumbling aloud over the lessons is an abomination, and ought to be eradicated. Noise during study-hours should not be tolerated. It is a mistake to suppose that students will become so interested in their lessons that their attention is not distracted by boisterous noise whether in class-recitation or elsewhere.

3. Regular Time for Study.—This is one of the essentials. The pupil who studies according to a programme, devoting a special time to each branch pursued, will accomplish more than he who studies irregularly as the mood may seize him. Study and rest should alternate. Short periods of study for small children are best. Indeed, short periods of study, less than an hour to each branch, are best for all pupils.

4. Variety in Study.—Study should not be continued on any branch for such a length of time as to weary the pupil. The most effective workers are they who alternate their work. When tired of one branch the pupil should turn to another as a rest, and when tired of this to still another, and so on, thus keeping up his interest and resting his mind by the variety. Hard study will do no one harm if he pursue a systematic plan which gives him sufficient variety of both study and recreation.

3. Helps to Study.

The pupil who relies on the textbook alone as his guide in study is apt to get only a partial view of the subject he pursues. Other aids are necessary to make his scholarship broad and comprehensive. The following are some of the important aids to study:

1. Other Textbooks.—Different authors present subjects in different lights and from different standpoints. The pupil will find it greatly to his advantage, therefore, to study a subject in various textbooks, using all of them to confirm the statements of the author he studies or gain new views and widen his field of knowledge.

2. Reference-Books.—Every school should be supplied with books of reference covering the school course of

study. These should include an unabridged Dictionary and a good Cyclopædia if possible. Even an abridged Cyclopædia will prove of great value to both pupils and teacher. To these should be added a Pronouncing Gazetteer, a Biographical Dictionary, and works on history, geography, science, and travel.

3. **Cabinets.**—These may be regarded in the light of objective helps. A cabinet contributed by the industry of the pupils will be useful. It should contain specimens of the various minerals, metals, grains, woods, leaves, grasses, etc. found in the vicinity of the school, or it would be better still if it contained specimens of all these found in the county. To this cabinet may be added curious or valuable specimens from different parts of the world; these will be found to add great interest and attractiveness to the collection.

4. **Apparatus.**—Good school apparatus, including sets of weights and measures, cubical blocks and other geometrical forms, will be found among the most useful helps to study.

4. Incentives to Study.

Pupils being surrounded by proper conditions, and having the desirable helps necessary to effective study, it is proper to state here the incentives or motives which should actuate them in the pursuit of knowledge. These incentives may be divided into two classes—*proper incentives* and *unwise incentives.*

Proper Incentives are such as may at all times be urged upon pupils without danger of doing harm to other members of the school. They are such as will promote the welfare of each pupil, but never at the expense or to the disadvantage of another. Among proper incentives the most important are—

1. The Approbation of Conscience.
2. The Approbation of the Teacher.
3. The Approbation of Parents and Friends.
4. The Desire of Acquiring Knowledge.
5. The Gratification of Curiosity.
6. The Pleasure of Overcoming Difficulties.
7. The Attainment of an Honorable Position in School.
8. The Hope of Success in Life.
9. The Approbation of Society.
10. The Duty of Self-Development.

1. The Approbation of Conscience.—The approval of one's own conscience is a strong incentive to proper effort, and no less so in the pursuit of knowledge than in the regulation of one's conduct. We do things because we believe them to be right, even when we do not stop to question the force of the obligation which impels us forward. It is always safe, therefore, for the teacher to appeal to the conscience of the child as a motive in urging him to diligent study.

2. The Approbation of the Teacher.—The pupil who does not desire to please the teacher, or who is not willing to do so, must have sunk to a low level indeed, and the teacher who does not command the respect and esteem of his pupils can certainly never exert a healthful influence over his school. We all desire the approbation of those for whom we labor, and a word of cheer or kindness from them will never fail to act as an incentive to more earnest effort.

The teacher who desires to secure the best work from his pupils must appreciate their work and give a word of praise where due. The oft-quoted rule, " Commend where you can, and censure only where you must," is a good one and a safe one to follow, both in the school-room and out of it. The teacher who is pleased with nothing, who is given to faultfinding or scolding instead of commendation, has passed his period of usefulness, and is no longer competent to do the teacher's work.

Indiscriminate praise, however, is not to be employed. The truthful teacher will not indulge in it. A kindly look or an approving nod when a pupil has done work deserving the attention and commendation of the teacher will always be appreciated by the child, and it will always have its due influence in urging him to greater diligence.

3. **The Approbation of Parents and Friends.**—The approbation of the parents and the friends of the pupil is also a proper incentive to study. Few parents, indeed, have so little love for their children that they are not anxious for them to succeed; and there are few children who are not anxious to win the commendation of both their parents and their friends for the excellence of their school work. The teacher will often be able to promote study by inviting the parents of pupils to visit the school for the purpose of inspecting its work.

4. **The Desire of Acquiring Knowledge.**—This is one of the strongest incentives to study. The desire for

knowledge is implanted in the child's nature. It eagerly seeks to learn, and it is left to the wisdom of the teacher to place before it such knowledge as is best fitted to give the mind the most symmetrical culture and development. The teacher may cultivate and strengthen this desire for knowledge by making his instruction interesting, and by giving to the child such facts as will lead him to investigate for himself the truths with which he comes in contact.

5. The Gratification of Curiosity.—Curiosity is characteristic of childhood. Little folks eagerly inquire, Why is this? what is the reason for that? The judicious teacher not only arouses curiosity, but he teaches also in a way to make children inquisitive and diligent to find out for themselves. Much of success in teaching lies in the ability to arouse the curiosity, the desire to know, on the part of children. The desire for knowledge once having been awakened, the work of teaching becomes easy. None are so easy to teach and so easy to manage as those who want to know.

The teacher should gratify the curiosity of children whenever it is possible to do so, but when he is unable to answer their questions he should not hesitate to tell them so. He deceives no one more than himself when he attempts to leave his pupils under the impression that he knows everything. New questions should be asked, and old questions should be put in a new way, so as to attract the attention and awaken the interest of the pupils. Thus through the very desire to gratify curiosity the pupil will arouse in himself an increased desire for knowledge.

6. **The Pleasure of Overcoming Difficulties.**—To the ambitious boy or girl probably no stronger incentive to study could be presented than the desire to come off victor in his contest with a mathematical problem or a complicated sentence in grammar. Children will run races, play at ball, jump, wrestle, etc. for the mere pleasure it gives them to vanquish some competitor or surmount some difficulty. The "puzzle" column in the weekly newspaper or the monthly magazine is frequently the most enticing department for young people. Nature implants this desire to test one's strength, in a mental as well as a physical sense, in the heart of every child.

The teacher, then, should make use of this characteristic in training the mind. Problems of such a character should be given as are not beyond the children's capacity, and yet sufficiently difficult to make them feel that they have something to contend with worthy of their strength. They should be encouraged to overcome these difficulties for themselves, and help should be given only when the ability of the child is found unequal to the task to be performed. Placing before pupils the biographies of such great men as have risen to eminence through their own contest with difficulties will greatly encourage the children and prompt them to do better work.

7. **The Attainment of an Honorable Position in School.** This as an incentive appeals directly to the self-respect of the pupil. Every one feels it an honor to stand high in his school and among the best in his class. Every pupil feels that it is worth years of hard mental

labor to be able to say that he was the best scholar in the school which he attended. This desire to attain an honorable position is an excellent incentive to study, and one that can be safely urged if care be taken that no one's success be based on another's downfall. Individual merit alone should be the basis of success.

8. The Hope of Success in Life.—The example of men who have succeeded in business or who have risen to distinction may safely be held before pupils as an incentive to study. The teacher should show that even an ordinary laborer or a mechanic succeeds better when educated to some extent, and that educated business-men of all kinds are those who are most successful, unless some weakness of character be present to prevent success. Educated men are the ones who are called upon to fill all important positions under the government. They are the men who take charge of our manufactories and railways, edit our newspapers, write our books, make our laws, preside over our courts, teach our schools, preach our sermons, and in general do the important work of the world.

9. The Approbation of Society.—Scholars stand higher in the esteem of every community than do the ignorant. Scholarship and education are admired even by those who do not possess them. The schoolboy who stands higher than his fellows is a source of pride to the community in which he lives, and is respected because of his knowledge. The approbation of the community, therefore, is a proper incentive to urge upon pupils to induce them to study.

10. **The Duty of Self-Development.**—This appeals to the conscience of the child, and as an incentive to study it can be used to advantage with older pupils only. The teacher should explain to his pupils the importance of securing a symmetrical development of both mind and body. He should show them how God has endowed them with certain mental faculties and physical powers which are designed to be perfected by use and training. They should be made to feel that they have the power within themselves thus to approximate perfection, and that it is their duty to aid the development of their mental and physical powers by proper study and exercise.

Unwise Incentives.

It is not argued that the following incentives are wholly improper at all times, but the doubt with which most of them are surrounded makes the propriety of ever using them at least questionable, if not unwise; and none but the weakest teachers will find it necessary to resort to their use. The following may be named as the chief incentives of this class:

1. Prizes.
2. Merit-Marks.
3. Personal Emulation.
4. Fear of Shame and Ridicule.
5. Scolding.
6. Fear of Punishment.

1. **Prizes.**—Under the head of prizes may be included anything of value—money, books, honors, etc.—which is offered to such as excel their schoolmates either in

study or in behavior. No doubt good is effected by offering prizes, but the question arises, Does not the evil engendered overbalance the good? We give the chief arguments on each side of the question.

The chief arguments in favor of prizes are—

1. **That the Expectation of Winning the Prize Induces the Pupil to Study more Diligently.**—It is certainly true that such pupils as have any prospect of winning the prize will strive more earnestly, at least for a time. If, in addition to study, general deportment is made one of the requisites for gaining the prize, still greater efforts will be made to win it, for here the difference in talent and the natural advantages of one pupil over another cannot have so much weight as where study or good recitations alone are made the criterion.

2. **That Profitable Competition is Promoted.**—It is argued that the efforts made by individuals to excel one another in a class strengthen each one, and that therefore the competition is profitable to those even who do not win, as well as to the more fortunate members who gain the honor. This is a strong argument in favor of prizes if the teacher be such as can manage the class properly and prevent jealousy and envy.

3. **That the Use of Prizes has Proved them Beneficial.**—It is claimed that the use of prizes has been continued so long in the shape of honors in our higher institutions, and in other forms in the lower, that certainly some good must be apparent or the system would long since have been abandoned.

The chief arguments against the use of prizes to promote study are—

1. **That the Benefits to be Derived are Limited to a Few Pupils.**—Were prizes offered to the whole school, graded according to actual merit, they would not be objectionable, but then they would be rewards of merit, and no longer prizes in the ordinary acceptation of the term. Prizes being limited to a few in number, however, the benefits of the system are also limited to those most likely to compete, and these, while they may at first constitute the whole class, decrease in number rapidly until there are but few more contestants than prizes.

2. **That Pupils are Injured rather than Benefited.**—The dull pupils, indeed all but the very brightest, soon become discouraged in the contest and relapse into greater lethargy than before, while the few participants who continue the contest are unduly stimulated, and thus have their powers overtaxed. Indeed, those who enter the contest for a prize are usually the pupils who require least stimulus, and who ought rather to be held back than urged.

3. **That Prizes Help to Disorganize the School.**—It is impossible to award prizes so as to please all. The usual result is, that those who fail in the contest become envious of the successful competitors, and the successful ones regard their less fortunate rivals with feelings no more praiseworthy. Discord is thus awakened, and the discipline of the school becomes much more difficult to maintain.

4. **That Prizes are Fictitious Rewards.**—They have no connection with study. The prize having been gained, there is nothing beyond, unless another prize be offered. The stimulus being withdrawn, the diligence no longer continues, and the pupil's habits of study are destroyed

rather than confirmed. The student having nothing but the prize in view overlooks the chief ends of study, and studies not to understand, not to learn, but to recite well and win the prize.

5. **That there is Difficulty in Awarding Prizes Justly.**— In awarding a prize the question at once arises, Shall it be on merit of recitation alone, or shall all incidental circumstances—the difference of natural talents, the home-surroundings, the age of the pupils, their advantages in securing outside help, etc.—be taken into consideration? Shall it be for scholarship alone, or shall deportment also be considered? Shall it be to those who study most industriously and recite but indifferently, or to those who, being talented, study but little, and yet make perfect recitations? These and many other questions arise in the very outstart, and to the teacher the act of awarding the prize to the most deserving is a matter of much perplexity.

6. **Great Harm is Frequently Done in Awarding Prizes.**— When recitation alone forms the basis of the award, merit in study is frequently overlooked. One child may have intelligent parents or brothers and sisters who can aid him in his study; he may have access to libraries, or he may have plenty of leisure, with nothing to distract his attention. All his surroundings are favorable to study. Another, equally talented, is placed in circumstances just the reverse. He finds no one at home to help him; he has no library to consult; much of his time is taken up in doing chores; his attention is distracted from study. These differences are not taken into consideration in awarding the prize, and the award is too often made to the less deserving of the two.

2. Merit-Marks.—Merit-marks have their use as an incentive to study. But to make them useful care must be taken to do exact justice to all. A system of marking in which a record is kept of every pupil's comparative success or failure in class-recitation will do much to create an interest in study, particularly among the older pupils. In this way also the school work may be better systematized, and the class-standing of pupils be determined more accurately than by any other.

The chief objections urged against merit-marks are—

1. That much Time is Consumed in Making the Record. —To this it may be answered that in most schools a sufficiently accurate record could be made at the close of each day, or even at the close of each week.

2. That Pupils Overlook Higher Objects of Study.—This, in a measure, is true, but by continued application the pupil will finally come to love study for its own sake. Merit-marks differ from prizes in being a continuous incentive.

Suggestion.—Never permit *demerits* to cancel *merit-marks*. When a pupil has earned a mark in recitation, let it be recorded in his favor. Marks for conduct should not be recorded against marks for recitation, nor should deficiency in one branch be made to detract from excellence in another. Each branch should be marked on its own merits. This is the only fair plan. To demerit a pupil for spelling in every branch recited is to demerit him as many times improperly as there are branches marked. Thus, to demerit him fifteen per cent. for spelling in each of five branches, and twenty-five per cent. in spelling itself, leaves him nothing whatever in that brqnch, whereas his true mark should be seven:y-five per cent.

3. **Personal Emulation.**—Emulation is properly the desire to surpass or excel others. It may be said of emulation as an incentive to study that its value depends entirely upon the spirit which influences the student in his pursuit of knowledge. If the spirit of emulation be such as to induce pupils to strive for success at the expense of others or by the downfall of others, it is reprehensible. But if the rivalry among schoolmates be generous, it may prove to be an excellent incentive + s⸱ ⸱dy. ⸱

This desire to surpass others and to excel is implanted in our nature. We all measure our own success by the success of others. Even in the games and plays of childhoo the same desire is always apparent. It is true we become in a measure ambitious, but the ambition is not necessarily harmful. Without this ambition to succeed the world would stagnate. All that ambition needs is to be wisely directed and controlled.

4. **Fear of Shame and Ridicule.**—This is not properly an incentive to study, nor should it ever be used. The pupil who can be reached by no more judicious or worthy incentive than this fear had better be dismissed. The teacher has no right to hold up any pupil to the ridicule of his fellows so long as that pupil can be reached in any other way. Nor is the result satisfactory. Funny mistakes may occur in classes, but the wise teacher never encourages laughter at the expense of the feelings of sensitive pupils.

5. **Scolding.**-- To scold pupils for failure in lessons is unwise. The best of pupils will in time become accustomed to scolding, and the heedless never care for it; so that in either case it has no good effect. It is difficult to see where any possible good can come from it. Pupils must in time lose respect for a scolding teacher.

6. **Fear of Punishment.**—This also is an unwise stimulus to study. The pupil who studies only because he expects punishment for failure will have but little love for learning. He may manage to recite well, but he can have no permanent interest in his work, and no permanent benefit should be expected from such enforced study. Fear of punishment may prevent wrong conduct, but good teaching ought never to need an incentive of this character.

5. How to Study.

One of the chief duties of the teacher is to train his pupils to correct habits of study, and thus make them self-dependent, that the best results may be attained. Study will thus be made interesting, the student will soon learn to help himself, and diligent study will become a life habit. The following *suggestions* will aid the student in systematizing the work of study.

1. **Read the Lesson Carefully.**—There are few branches of study in which it will not be to the advantage of the pupils for the teacher to read over the lesson slowly and carefully before assigning it for study, so that every idea may be developed and be grasped by the pupil. Words not familiar should be expressed in simpler language, and principles not clearly explained should be made clear,

that the pupil may be enabled to study the subject un-derstandingly.

2. The Essentials of the Lesson.—The teacher should point out the essential parts of the lesson and call attention to them. Some parts of a lesson may profitably be read which it would be useless to commit and attempt to hold in the mind, while the main principles and the important definitions should claim the closest study and attention. The teacher in reading over the lesson should discriminate as to these, that the child may not waste either energy or time.

3. A Clear Idea of the Lesson.—Having examined the lesson in detail, the teacher should give the pupil a clear idea of the topic treated as a whole. The pupil will thus apply each individual fact that illustrates the general idea, and study each principle with that general idea constantly in view.

4. Primary Study must be Inductive.—The student should be trained to pursue the study of any subject inductively—that is, from the particular facts to the general laws or principles. Particulars should be illustrated, and the illustrations should be so simple that the learner must understand. The general rule or law should be given only when the individual cases and their application to the general principle are fully understood.

5. Pupils must Study Understandingly.—The teacher must be careful to see that pupils do not commit to memory definitions, principles, or rules without first understanding their full meaning. Each rule or principle should be clearly understood by the student, and he should be able to illustrate each one intelligently. In such studies as geometry or grammar pupils are partic-

ularly liable to commit to memory the subject-matter of the book without a clear comprehension of the meaning of the words of the book.

6. **Pupils should Study Alone.**—We grow not by what others do for us, but by what we do for ourselves. Self-help is the only means by which we acquire power and development. Assistance is of course well meant, but a pupil never should accept it, even from a teacher, when it is in his power to perform his own mental labor. Independent study leads to independent thought and action and intellectual strength.

7. **Study by Outline.**—Pupils should be taught to outline or synopsize the topics they study. The synopsis will not only train them to be systematic, and show that they have a comprehensive view of the subject, but it will also aid the memory, and enable the pupils to comprehend the relation between the various divisions of a subject.

8. **Thought must be Concentrated.**—The pupil who permits his thoughts to wander to a number of topics while engaged in the study of a special one will rarely accomplish much. To study effectively, the mind must be devoted to one thing at a time, and the more intense the application the more effective, as a rule, will be the study.

6. Attention.

Attention is that general power by which the mind directs its thoughts voluntarily to some one object to the exclusion of others. Without the aid of attention no mental labor could be performed. On it depends the activity of each of the distinct mental faculties.

Without it there could be no study. The importance, therefore, of securing habits of attention is evident. Among the requisites for securing attention the following are important:

1. **The Teacher must be Interesting.**—The minister who interests his congregation or the orator who interests his audience never finds his hearers inattentive. For the same reason, the teacher who interests his pupils not only finds them easily controlled, but he also holds their attention and induces them to study. The facts presented by the teacher should be interesting. The curiosity of the pupils should be aroused, and the knowledge communicated should be of such a character as to create a desire for more on the part of the pupil.

2. **The Teacher should be Animated in Manner.**—The dull, heavy, plodding teacher never can expect to create much interest in study, and the same is true of the teacher who finds it necessary to refer constantly to the textbook to determine the correctness or incorrectness of a pupil's answer. In order to succeed, particularly with small children, the teacher must be active, wide-awake, and energetic.

3. **The Teacher should Present that which is New.**—The child is always on the lookout for something novel. Its curiosity is implanted in its nature for a wise purpose. Great interest may be awakened by placing before it new objects which it can examine for itself, and presenting new truths with which to arouse thought.

4. **Stories and Anecdotes should be Used in Teaching.**—Children are always awake to the power of illustration by stories. The dry details and facts of knowledge

may be made tenfold more interesting by associating with them anecdotes, vivid descriptions, or stories.

5. **The Teacher should Adapt his Teaching to the Capacity of his Pupils.**—The teacher's language must be such as his pupils can comprehend, and his illustrations such as they will readily understand. His manner also must be adapted to the age and capacity of the children.

6. **The Teacher should Attract Attention by Good Elocution.**—Pleasant tones of voice, sufficiently distinct, but not too loud, should be used in the school-room. Pupils are attentive when natural tones are used. Fretful or noisy speech irritates them, and interferes greatly with their study. Monotone interests them but little more than do the constant buzz and hum of machinery, but lively, sparkling, conversational tones are always attractive.

7. **The Teacher should not Talk too Much.**—He should talk to the point, and say only what is necessary. Much talking, and particularly useless talking, distracts the attention of pupils. One statement to pupils, one reading of a question, one pronunciation of a word in a spelling class, ought to be sufficient. The teacher ought not to encourage inattentive pupils by repetition.

8. **The Teacher should Hold Attention by good Class Management.**—Let the class feel that any member is liable to be called upon at any moment to recite. Nothing can be more unsatisfactory than a plan of recitation by which the teacher calls on his class-members to recite in alphabetic order or in the order in which they are seated. The pupils soon catch the trick, and prepare themselves only when they expect to recite.

9. **Inattentive Pupils should be Called Frequently to**

Recite.--This will train them to give their attention during the recitation. Those also who are inclined to interest themselves during recitation in matters foreign to the lesson should be called upon whenever their attention wanders. Persistence in this plan will cure the worst cases.

10. The Teacher should Hold Attention by Variety in Exercises.—He who knows but one method of presenting a subject, or but one means of conducting a recitation, is prepared for his work poorly indeed. He is much in the position of a physician who always prescribes the same medicine to all his patients. The true teacher should be prepared to put his statements in a variety of ways, so as to adapt himself to the wants and understanding of every pupil.

11. The Teacher should be Vigilant, and Keep his Pupils Vigilant.—If the members of a class become inattentive because the teacher interests himself in one or a few, or from any other cause, the recitation should be discontinned at once, and not be resumed until all become orderly and attentive. If a pupil be stubbornly inattentive, it is best either to ignore him during that recitation or dismiss him from the class for the time. It is useless to convince him of his wrong when in the kind of humor which makes him stubborn and disobedient.

12. The Teacher should Show his Pupils that Attention is the Condition of Success.—Their attention should be called to successful citizens—merchants, mechanics, and professional men—who have won success by giving attention to business and doing their work well. Illustrate to them, by notable examples from history— Newton, Scott, Dickens, Bryant, Napoleon, etc.—that

prolonged attention wins success. Train them t(
into their own life and there see the importance
value of forming habits of attention in order to make
them successful. ˙Mental strength is to a great extent
the result of continued attention.

The following brief Suggestions are made to teachers
with the view of aiding them in securing and holding
the attention of their pupils:

1. Have your pupils observe closely.

2. Arouse their curiosity.

3. Show that you yourself ·are interested in their
work.

4. Be cheerful.

5. Vary your methods of recitation.

6. Use the textbook as little as possible.

7. Let vour position before the class be such that you
can look every pupil in the eye.

8. Read a story or a description occasionally, and then
have it reproduced by the pupils, either orally or in
writing.

9. Show your pupils that you expect to have them
ready to reproduce at any time whatever you may tell
them in recitation.

10. Cultivate attention by giving proper praise and
credit when pupils are attentive.

7· Rules for Study.

The following condensed directions for study may
assist both student and teacher :

1. **Try to be Interested.**—We make little progress in a
study which has no interest for us.

2. **Study to Know.**—The difficulty with many pupils

is that they study for the recitation. They commit to memory where they ought simply to try to comprehend. The result is that they forget readily, and their work is fruitless.

3. **Give Close Attention.**—Close attention and close observation are necessary to give clear perception. Close attention is necessary also to strengthen the memory, and thus enable us to retain knowledge and recall it at will.

4. **Study Systematically.**—Master each point as you go. See that each principle is understood before you study the next that depends on it. Go from the known to the unknown. Make an effort to comprehend everything as it comes to you in turn, so that when you finish a book you understand everything in it. Systematic study will save much valuable time. Systematize your time also in such a way as will give to each study its due proportion.

5. **Use your Knowledge.**—We know a thing better after we have told it to another. We know it still better after we have written about it. Nothing so firmly fixes the knowledge in our minds as the attempt to communicate it to others. This is one of the chief objects of the class-recitation, to get such a clear comprehension of what we learn that we can tell it to others.

6. **Think.**—It is the man who thinks that makes his mark in the world. Be sure of your knowledge. Think for yourself. If you can give a different solution or a different demonstration from that of your teacher or the book, give it. Do not let a word or a definition pass without comprehending its meaning fully. The men who think clearly, quickly, and independently are the

ones whom the world recognizes as the great men who are its masters.

7. **Alternate Study and Recreation.**—The bow always bent loses its elasticity. The mind constantly kept at hard work must ultimately be weakened. Study and recreation must alternate, that work may be performed advantageously. Periods of study and relaxation judiciously intermingled will greatly aid students in mastering subjects, but constant study will prove of but little more permanent benefit than constant play. Mental recreation is quite as necessary as physical recreation.

II. Recitation.

The recitation is an important feature of school management. Here the teacher tests the work of his pupils and ascertains their progress. Here he guides and directs their powers, arouses their enthusiasm, and inspires them by his example. Here he measures their minds, and determines the help that may be necessary to make them successful students.

1. The Objects of the Recitation.

The chief objects of the recitation are—

1. The Mental Discipline of the Pupil.
2. Instruction Imparted by the Teacher.

To these may be added the following subordinate objects:

3. To Enable Pupils to Express themselves Properly.
4. To Enable Pupils to Gain Self-Confidence.
5. To Enable Pupils to Fix in their Minds what they Learn.

6. To Awaken Interest in Study.

7. To Make Pupils Inquisitive.

8. To Cultivate Habits of Attention.

9. To Enable the Teacher to Correct Errors.

10. To Enable the Teacher to Test the Preparation of the Lesson.

1. The Mental Discipline of the Pupil.—So far as the pupil is concerned, this is the chief object of the recitation. Private students, however diligent they may be in the pursuit of knowledge, never receive that culture and discipline of mind which come only from the competition of classmates in the daily recitation. None of us are quite sure we know a truth until we come to tell it. We may think our comprehension clear, but there is no certainty until we apply the test. Every recitation develops mental power on the part of attentive pupils.

2. Instruction Imparted by the Teacher.—This also is an important object of the recitation. The teacher who can ask only the printed questions of the textbook is not a teacher, and the one who can impart no additional instruction to that given in the textbook is but little better qualified to teach. It is the business of the teacher to impart instruction aside from that found in the book. It is his duty to make that of the book comprehended by the pupils. The best teachers are those who bring themselves to the level of the child-mind, and then put the knowledge to be imparted in such shape as will enable the learner to grasp it most readily. Here is the teacher's opportunity—not only to add new and important facts, but also to give moral instruction in an incidental way, and guide and direct the child's

powers in such a manner as to give the most symmetrical development.

3. **The Recitation Gives Culture in Language.**—It is
important that the pupil should be able to tell what he
knows, and tell it in good language. Nothing is of so
much help to him in this respect as the class-recitation.
It is no easy thing to think clearly while on one's feet.
Daily practice, however, will enable all pupils in time to
express themselves clearly and accurately. This is true
of the written recitation also. It is wonderful how rapidly pupils improve in composition and the use of language by frequent written recitations.

4. **The Class-Recitation Gives the Pupil Self-Confidence.**—
The men who can rise before an audience and give their
opinions calmly and intelligently are comparatively few
in number. Indeed, it is true of many of our ablest
scholars that they find great difficulty in speaking before an audience, and this because of their lack of confidence in their ability to do so. Class-recitation will not
only in a great measure overcome this, but with proper
criticism it will also help to repress the tendency man-
ifested by some to speak too much.

5. **The Recitation Helps to Fix in the Mind of the Child
what he Learns.**—We know a fact more thoroughly after
we have told it to another. Indeed, the very effort to retain it in the memory in order that we may tell it helps to
strengthen that mental faculty, and helps to impress the fact
on the mind. Every repetition of it also serves to make
the impression all the deeper. Even the private student
will find it to his advantage to tell his knowledge to his
friends, or, in their absence, to the furniture in his room
as imaginary schoolfellows.

6. **The Recitation Awakens an Interest in Study.**—Class competition creates interest. In general, the smallest classes are those most difficult to interest. But in medium-sized classes, where there is a chance for every one to test his ability and compete with the other class-members, and where the criticism of both teacher and pupils is of such a character as to keep all vigilant and active, interest in study rises to its maximum. The additional knowledge imparted by the teacher during recitation will also add greatly to the interest of the child ; and thus study will be pursued with greater eagerness and under the most favorable conditions.

7. **The Class-Recitation will Make Pupils Inquisitive.**— This being true, they will be better prepared to receive such instruction as the teacher may be able to impart. Having become inquisitive and desirous of knowing, the child places himself in the best possible of teachable conditions, and he will be led to search for knowledge and think for himself—an end greatly to be desired in all teaching.

8. **The Recitation Cultivates Habits of Attention.**—No matter how heedlessly a pupil may have conned over his lesson while preparing it, the moment he enters the recitation he feels that his attention must be given not only to his own assigned work, but also to that of his classmates and to the questions and instruction of the teacher. However negligent he may be elsewhere, here he must be attentive, and the influence exerted on him here will also be felt elsewhere.

9. **The Recitation Enables the Teacher to Correct Errors.** —The correction of pupils' mistakes by the teacher is a recognized duty. If the pupils are competent and the

criticism be kind, they should be permitted to correct one another's errors; but in the event of their failure to do so, it becomes the duty of the teacher to be watchful and make all proper corrections. Many errors never can be detected except in class-recitation: this is true particularly of errors in pronunciation.

10. The Recitation Enables the Teacher to Test the Work Done by the Pupils.—Judicious questioning and judicious methods of conducting the recitation will enable the teacher in a very short time to detect the idle as well as the studious in the class. Thus day by day also he will be able to determine which students are diligent and which otherwise. He will be able also to determine by the daily recitation not only the relative improvement of the class-members, but also the improvement of the class as a whole. He thus becomes prepared from day to day to assign work in advance, of such a nature and in such quantity as will give his pupils healthy mental and moral growth. The difficulties can be so simplified as to bring them within the mental grasp of the pupil, and such incentives can be placed before the child as will arouse in him increased vigor and create a desire to culture himself to the utmost.

2. Methods of Recitation.

The methods of conducting class-recitations are many, and each has its excellence. The ingenious teacher will never fail to adapt his method to both the subject taught and the peculiarities of his pupils. It may be said, however, that sometimes this is a delicate task. We mention here only the most important methods. They are—

1. The Socratic Method.
2. The Topical Method.
3. The Question Method.
4. The Discussion Method.
5. The Conversational Method.
6. The Oral or Lecture Method.

1. The Socratic Method.—The Socratic, named from the Grecian philosopher Socrates, is that in which the pupil is led by means of judicious questions to discover truth for himself. The teacher so shapes his questions as to lead his pupils to think for themselves, and thus gain knowledge by their own effort. By this method the teacher acts constantly as a guide, but he imparts little, and that little only where the pupil is unable to help himself. In a similar manner the pupil is led to discover his own errors, and is thus placed in a position to correct them.

Illustration.—The following will illustrate briefly the Socratic method :

Teacher (who is desirous of showing the relation of a surface one foot square to that of one three feet square). If I draw a square whose base is one foot, how large is the figure?

Pupil. One foot square, or it is a square foot.

Teacher. If now I draw a line a yard long, and on it construct a square, how large will the figure be?

Pupil. A yard square, or three square feet.

Teacher. Is there, then, no difference between a yard square and three square feet?

Pupil. None.

Teacher. Let us draw the figures.

The pupil, under the teacher's direction, draws a figure a foot square and one a yard square, and then divides the larger figure into nine equal smaller squares.

Teacher. Examine these squares; how large is cach?

Pupil. Each is a foot square, or a square foot.

Teacher. How many are there?

Pupil. There are nine, sir.

Teacher. How many square feet, then, does a square yard contain?

Pupil. Nine square feet.

Teacher. Then, what is the difference between three feet square and three square feet?

Pupil. A figure three feet square contains nine square feet; it is therefore three times as large as three square feet, or nine times as large as one square foot.

Teacher. That is correct.

Advantages.—The great advantages of the Socratic method are, that pupils glean knowledge for themselves, and thus in overcoming obstacles and surmounting difficulties win their own victories. Every victory gained is enjoyed, and the battle makes the pupil the stronger. The knowledge acquired is of such an interesting nature that the impression on the child's mind is strong, and therefore lasting. This method makes the pupil the worker, but the work is enjoyable, and therefore but little is demanded from the teacher except judicious guidance. Its sphere lies mostly in the primary or lower-grade schools.

2. The Topical Method.—This consists in assigning to as many of the pupils as possible each an individual topic for recitation. Each may be required to tell all he

can about the topic assigned, or he may be closely questioned on the topic, or both methods may be combined.

Advantages.—The advantages of this method are that it trains pupils to study by topics, rather than for the purpose of answering questions; it also enables the pupil to gain culture in language by making his statements in connected discourse; and it affords an opportunity to conduct a written and an oral recitation at the same time.

Disadvantages.—There is danger that the matter of imparting instruction may be crowded out, and the time of the class be used wholly in reciting. Pupils may prepare themselves only on the topics most readily recited. Habits of attention may be destroyed unless the teacher is careful to assign topics frequently to those most likely to be inattentive, or judiciously mingle questions with the topics.

3. The Question Method.—This is known also as the "Question-and-Answer Method." It is the one in general use. It differs from the true Socratic method in this—that it makes no effort to search for new truth, or even to correct error. It simply catechizes the pupil on the subject-matter of the lesson, and this mostly for the purpose of testing his preparation.

Advantages.—Questioning is an art which, when judiciously used, will serve a good purpose, not only in testing the pupil's knowledge, but also in arousing thought. One of the chief advantages is that the teacher can not only ascertain the pupil's preparation, but also detect any errors which the learner may have imbibed. He is enabled also to select only the essential points, passing over those of minor importance.

Abuse.—No method is more liable to abuse. The inexperienced teacher always adopts this method, partly because it is easy to ask questions, and partly because he knows of no better. When printed questions occur in the book, he is apt to confine himself to these, and rest satisfied if the answers of the book be given correctly. But little if any effort is made to impart instruction; and the pupil comes to think that when he has answered all the book-questions by the book-answers, he is a finished scholar in that branch of study.

4. The Discussion Method.—This method consists of a statement of opinion by each pupil on the question to be discussed, with the reasons for holding that opinion. It is a method which can be used in only a portion of the branches taught, except in an incidental way. It may be used wherever there is room for difference of opinion. Incidental questions spring up in connection with almost every branch of study which may profitably be made subjects of discussion.

Advantages.—This method develops thought. It acts as an incentive to the thorough preparation of the lesson, and also induces the student to search for knowledge beyond that furnished by the textbook or even by the teacher. The student not only gleans the facts, but also receives culture in the use of language as he states them in the most forcible and convincing way. His thoughts clarify, and when he expresses them he makes an effort to put them in the most pointed language.

Abuse.—There is danger that some may talk too much, or that the talk may not be to the point. There is danger also that trivial topics may become the basis of discussion, and valuable time be thus squandered. Sometimes, also, the debate may run to personalities, and the feelings of some be wounded. The teacher must exercise great caution that none of these be permitted to mar the pleasure or interfere with the profit of the recitation.

5. The Conversational Method.—This resembles the discussion method. The teacher, however, here takes part, and expresses his opinions also. In truth, the pupils spend the time mostly in asking questions, while the teacher explains and answers. This method may be employed in almost every class to some extent, and it will always be found of advantage where pupils are wide awake and anxious to learn. The teacher permits all relevant questions to be asked, and answers to the best of his ability. The teacher may also ask such questions as naturally grow out of the lesson.

Advantages.—This method is of special advantage where professional instruction is to be imparted, as in normal schools, medical colleges, etc., but it is of advantage also in every other school in which the teacher is a man of scholarship. Pupils may often learn more from a genial and scholarly teacher than from textbooks. This method of recitation has the advantage also of giving students that knowledge which they most desire, and that which it is most important for them to possess.

Abuse.—There is danger in the use of the conversational method that many questions may be asked which do not relate to the subject of the lesson, or the teacher may be too talkative and himself wander away from the topic. There is danger also that the pupils may set the teacher to talking, as wise college-boys often have done, for the purpose of avoiding the recitation of the day. Teachers who attempt to use the conversational method must feel that they have the knowledge necessary to keep up the proper interest in class.

6. The Lecture Method.—This consists in the teacher's presenting and discussing a subject, while the pupils sit and listen and attempt to fix in their minds the leading points, to be reproduced at some future time.

A variation of the method consists in having the pupils take notes, which are to form the basis for future study.

A second variation consists in having the teacher submit simply an outline of the subject, and at the same time suggest the best method of study and the proper books to be consulted.

Advantage.—The chief advantage of this method lies in the fact that the lecturer can reach an audience of hundreds at the same time, and thus present his knowledge without increased effort to a much larger number than by any other method.

Abuse.—The method has many disadvantages and dangers. Only those most closely attentive receive any benefit. Even universities and professional schools find it necessary to have frequent examinations on the subject-matter of the lectures, in order to derive any benefit from the lecture method. The lecturer is unable to determine who of his audience comprehend his statements. Much repetition is necessary, that the few grains of wheat in the large quantity of mental chaff may be safely lodged in the mind of the learner.

In the lower-grade schools the lecture method has no

place whatever. It is worse than useless, and as a distinctive method in the higher-grade schools it has but little value unless associated with some of the more valuable methods. The chief value of oral instruction, as distinguished from the lecture method of recitation, is found in primary schools, where object-lessons form the basis of instruction.

A Combination of Methods, and the frequent use of the most valuable parts of each, will produce the best results. The progressive and earnest teacher finds it necessary to vary his methods constantly, so as to keep up the greatest possible interest.

3. The Art of Questioning.

Questioning is an important part of every valuable method of recitation, and the teacher who best understands the art of questioning will in general succeed best, not only in awakening interest, but also in discipline and in imparting knowledge.

Objects of Questioning.

1. The first important object of questioning is **to give proper direction to the efforts of the learner.** Few pupils know how to pursue a study to the best advantage. A few judicious questions from the teacher will give his pupils the key, and thus enable them to gain knowledge by their own independent effort. This is the valuable feature of the Socratic method of imparting knowledge, that it induces the pupil, under the guidance of the teacher, to search for truth for himself.

2. An important object of questioning is **to detect and correct error.** Pupils do not always study understand-

ingly. Frequently they commit words, but fail to acquire ideas. Often their comprehension is not clear or their view is but a partial one. To many a pupil a circle means the curved line, and not the space enclosed within. All these errors' can be best reached by judicious questions. The teacher should never rest satisfied when the pupil gives the mere textbook answer, but he should see that the child's comprehension of that answer is clear and correct.

3. An important object of questioning is **to test the preparation of the lesson.** There is danger that a pupil may prepare his lesson only when he expects to be called on to recite; but when he feels that the teacher is liable to call on him at any time or any number of times during a recitation, the danger is obviated, because he makes preparation for every recitation.

4. It is an important object of questioning **to bring out the essentials of a lesson.** Often that which is of least importance in a topic, as the illustrations and anecdotes, will be found to be that which is most readily remembered by the pupil. Judicious questioning will show the pupil the application of these and impress the principle on the child's mind.

5. It is an object of questioning **to cultivate attention.** Next to the interest aroused by apt oral instruction, nothing is so well calculated to keep awake the attention of a class as judicious questioning. The thoughtful teacher will of course see that all pupils are questioned, not in consecutive order, but promiscuously, and particularly when least attentive.

6. It is an object of questioning **to train pupils to think.** The teacher who does not arouse thought in the

minds of his pupils fails in an important part of his work. This is indeed one of the chief objects of all education—to make thinkers. Questions should be so put as to lead pupils to think for themselves. Having once been trained to think and reflect, the pupil learns for himself, and the truths he discovers become his own.

How to Put Questions.

1. **A Question may be Put to the Whole Class.**—The advantage in this method is that the attention of all the pupils is necessary. Various plans may be followed as to the manner of receiving the answer

a. The pupils may be permitted to think for a moment, and then some particular one be called upon for an answer.

b. When the question is put, all that are able to answer may be permitted to raise the hand, and then the teacher selects some one to recite.

c. Some one may be called upon to answer in part, and suddenly another member of the class may be directed to finish the answer.

d. The answer may be given in concert.

2. **The Question may be Put to a Single Member of the Class.**—This plan also has its advantages, and the attention of all may be secured almost as well as by putting the question to the whole class. Several variations of this plan may be followed:

a. When one pupil has partially answered a question, another may be called upon to finish it.

b. A pupil may be called upon to answer not only the first question propounded, but also such others as may naturally follow.

c. A pupil having answered his question, as an occasional exercise may be accorded the privilege of putting a question to some other member of the class.

Cautions.—The following cautions are important:

1. Do not question your pupils in alphabetical order.

2. Do not question your pupils in the order in which they are seated.

3. Do not fall into the habit of permitting your pupils to answer in concert.

4. Do not help your pupils to answer by suggesting an important word here and there.

5. Do not depend on the textbook for question and answer.

6. Ask your questions promiscuously.

7. Frequently call upon the inattentive to answer.

8. If some pupils remain inattentive, keep on asking them questions, even if they receive the greater part of lesson.

9. Put your questions in proper tones of voice.

10. Do not scold a pupil for failure to answer.

11. Rarely repeat a question. Your pupils should be attentive and hear it the first time.

12. Always give your slow pupils time to think. Pupils vary greatly in their ability to express themselves promptly.

13. Put your questions so as to make your pupils discover truth for themselves.

14. Encourage your pupils to ask questions, and when you have time let other pupils answer.

15. When you make an explanation, see that your pupils understand it, and then call upon some of them to repeat it.

The Subject-Matter of Questions.

1. **The Questions should be Definite.**—Obscurity in the language of a question may lead to incorrect answers, for which the teacher and not the pupil is responsible. Questions should be pointed, and so definite in meaning that the pupil will not fail to understand.

2. **Questions should be Pertinent.**—They should relate to the subject. Irrelevant questions, or such as do not pertain to the lesson, should not be given, though the teacher will do well at any time to test the pupil's general knowledge by asking questions which are not answered by the statements of the textbook.

3. **Questions should be Exhaustive.**—The teacher should see that every part of the lesson is understood. He can best do this by making his questions exhaustive in character, so that they may cover the entire ground of the lesson.

4. **The Questions should be Graded.**—It is wise to grade the difficulty of the question according to the capacity of the pupil. There will be some in the class who can answer every question, while others think more slowly and find greater difficulty in expressing themselves. The teacher may venture on giving to the former any question, but it may be necessary to encourage the slower pupil by giving him frequently some of the easier work to perform.

Cautions.—1. Do not put questions to puzzle pupils.

2. Do not put irrelevant questions to show your own learning.

3. Do not put questions that include too much.

4. Do not put silly questions.

5. Do not put aimless questions.

6. Do not put questions whose language is ambiguous.

The Forms of Questions.

1. **Questions should be Concise.**—The language of the question should be concise and express briefly what is required. This is particularly true of oral questions. Too often in attempting to keep in mind the wording of a question the pupils lose the idea.

2. **Questions should be Clearly Stated.**—The language should be such that the pupil may understand just what is required of him. The language should also be precise, so that the exact meaning may be expressed.

3. **Questions should be Adapted to the Subject.**—Questions in grammar must necessarily differ in form from those given in geography or arithmetic, and thus, in general, each branch of study must have the form of questions adapted so as best to develop the thought and test the knowledge of the learner.

4. **Questions should be Varied in Form,** so as to keep up interest in the work. That teacher usually succeeds best who by constantly varying his manner of instructing and questioning keeps up the most lively interest in his class; and he who falls into the monotonous routine of presenting his questions all in the same form must eventually find his pupils becoming dull and listless.

Cautions.—1. Do not use leading questions; as, "Paris is in France, is it not?"

2. Do not put questions that can be answered by *yes* or *no.*

3. Do not put questions which are alternate in form; as, "Is Presque Isle an island or not?"

4. Do not put questions in such a form as to suggest the answer; as, "Was Washington the first President of the United States?"

The Manner of Putting Questions.

Variety is necessary in the matter of conducting class-recitations, that the interest of pupils may be kept fully aroused. The teacher should change his manner from day to day. The following methods will prove of advantage:

1. Give the question in a general way to the whole class before calling on any particular one to recite.

2. Sometimes permit the pupils to ask the questions while you recite.

3. Sometimes put all the questions to a single pupil or two.

4. When conveying instruction, lead pupils to discover error as well as truth by such questions as will lead them to think.

5. When testing knowledge, put the questions in such a way as to draw out the full understanding of the pupil.

6. Sometimes allow a pupil to take the place of the teacher in asking questions of his fellows.

7. Permit pupils to ask all the questions they desire, so long as they seek for information.

8. Be prompt to repress any questions asked for mere pertness or a desire to puzzle.

4. Answers.

Answers must of course conform to the questions asked, and they must be governed to some extent by the same principles that apply to questions. The following suggestions are submitted:

1. **The Answers should be to the Point.**—They should contain all that is implied in the questions, but no more.

2. **They should be Concise.**—No more words should be used than are necessary to express the thought definitely.

3. **They should be Clear.**—The language of the answer should not be ambiguous or liable to misconstruction.

4. **They should be Comprehensive.**—A partial answer is not sufficient. The answer should be full and cover all that is called for by the question.

5. **They should be Given Understandingly.**—The pupil should not be permitted to commit an answer to memory and repeat it without fully understanding it.

6. **They should be Correct.**—This is true of both the answer itself and the language in which it is expressed. Errors either in fact or in language should be corrected. Errors of fact may be corrected by the pupils, but errors in language are generally best corrected by the teacher.

7. **They should be Given in Proper Tones of Voice.**— Neither a monotonous drawl nor a high-pitched, rapid enunciation should be permitted. Pleasant conversational tones are the best suited to school-room work.

8. **They should Usually be Given Singly.**—Concert recitations are not well calculated to test knowledge, however well adapted they may be for the purpose of drill.

9. **They may be Given Orally or in Writing.**—Both methods have their advantages. A change from one method to the other is frequently advantageous. It is a good plan also to have a portion of the class engaged in writing answers while others answer orally to a different set of questions.

9

10. With Beginners the Answers should be in Complete Sentences.—This will be of valuable aid to them in giving them language-culture, but it should not be carried to extremes.

11. The Mode of Answering must be Adapted to the Character of the Study.—Thus, the parsing of a word, the analysis of a sentence, the solution of a problem, the discussion of a topic in history, the reading of a paragraph, and the answer to a question in geography,—all must differ somewhat in form.

5. Criticism.

Error in answers should be corrected in class. The corrections may be made by either the pupils or the teacher. When possible, the pupil should be permitted to correct his own errors. If the pupils are permitted to make the corrections, they will become more observant of their own mistakes. This plan also cultivates attention and makes each one watchful.

Criticism should be Kindly in its Character.—Criticism for the mere purpose of finding fault or exhibiting a pupil's smartness should not be tolerated. Much injury may be done to a diffident pupil by sharp and uncalled-for criticism.

Criticism should be Discriminative.—A mere slip of the tongue or a slight error in pronunciation is sometimes deemed of more importance in the mind of the critic than a misstatement of fact. Criticism of this kind should be repressed. Care should be taken that timid pupils be not discouraged by harsh or unwise criticism.

Criticism should Point out Merits as well as Demerits.— Great care must be taken, however, that pupils do not

fall into the habit of overpraising or praising indiscrim-
inately. Such praise soon loses its effect. To say of
each pupil as he recites, " You did well," becomes monotonous in the extreme, and quite as untruthful as
monotonous.

**Criticism should be Made with the Purpose of Conveying
Information.**—Where there is danger that criticism by
pupils may be unkind or undiscriminating in its character, the teacher should correct the mistakes, and in doing
so lead the pupils, when possible, to discover their own
errors and correct them.

6. Preparation for the Recitation.

I. The Teacher.

**1. The Teacher should Prepare each Lesson by Fresh
Study.**—No matter how well he may understand the
subject, new study will suggest new ideas and new
methods of illustration, by means of which the lesson
may be made more interesting and profitable.

**2. The Teacher must be Familiar with the Subject-
matter of the Lesson.**—We cannot teach that which we
do not know. A teacher may possibly suggest methods
of study in branches with which he is not thoroughly
familiar, but he surely cannot teach those branches, nor
any part of them, profitably unless he thoroughly understands them.

**3. The Teacher Needs Preparation, that he may Add to the
Knowledge supplied by the Textbook.**—A textbook is, after
all, a mere outline of the study to be pursued. Many
facts are to be added, many explanations of principles
are demanded, many illustrations are to be given, that

the pupil may fully understand and comprehend his work. Hearing a lesson recited is not teaching. Teaching in its proper sense demands close study on the part of the teacher, that he may illustrate and explain, and thus interest and instruct.

4. The Teacher Needs Preparation, that he may Present the Facts and Truths of the Lesson in their Proper Order. —The natural order, or that in which pupils will most readily grasp the truth, will be found the best in which to present it. A heterogeneous mixture of disconnected facts is almost valueless as knowledge.

5. The Teacher Needs Preparation, that he may be Able to Show clearly the Relation of each Lesson to its Predecessor.—Lessons cannot be profitably taught except as they sustain and strengthen one another. The principles and truths of science are valuable mainly through their relations. Disconnect them, and they become a mere mass of disjointed fragments which have no relation except in their application.

6. The Teacher Needs Preparation, that he may Have at Command the Entire Subject-matter of the Lesson.—Nothing will so confuse a teacher as to have his pupils drive sharp questions at him when he is unprepared to answer; and nothing will so soon cause pupils to lose confidence in that teacher as finding him unable to give them the information they seek. Everything with reference to the lesson should be clear in his mind, that he may be able to give information when it is desired.

7. The Teacher Needs Preparation, that he may be Enabled to Present the Difficulties of the Lesson in an Intelligible Manner.—The language of the textbook may be obscure or the comprehension of a pupil in a measure dull. It

is for the teacher to explain the textbook in such terms as the dullest pupil can comprehend. Clear language needs clear thought, and clear thought needs clear language in which to express it.

8. **The Teacher Needs Preparation, that he may be Able to Conduct the Recitation without Loss of Time.**—Where apparatus is needed it should be in place before the recitation begins. No time ought to be lost in hunting or putting in place charts, maps, or other apparatus. The same may be said of subsidiary questions likely to come up in the lesson. There is no more pitiful sight than that of a teacher who knows so little of a lesson that he is compelled to hunt for the answer to his question while the pupil is attempting to give it orally.

2. The Pupil.

The chief object of the assignment of lessons is that pupils may both gain discipline of mind and acquire knowledge while preparing to recite. This end is frequently neither understood nor appreciated by either teacher or pupil, and too often the preparation of the lesson is made simply for the purpose of reciting well and securing a high standing in class. The importance of the pupil's preparation of the lesson seems so obvious that it needs no argument. The following are the chief *reasons* why pupils should make preparation for recitation :

1. The pupil must study the lesson in order that he may acquire knowledge.

2. He must study the lesson in order that he may express himself clearly.

3. He must study the lesson in order that he may

seek information on points which he does not fully understand.

4. He must study the lesson in order that he may
fully understand the relation between the principles of
the branch studied.

5. He must study the lesson in order to gain discipline.

6. He must study that his knowledge may become
systematized in his mind.

7. He must study that he may make the truths presented by the textbook or taught by the teacher a part
of his own knowledge.

8. He should seek as little help as possible from either
his teacher or his associates.

7. The Teacher in the Recitation.

The success of the recitation depends much upon the
manner in which the teacher conducts his work. A hasty,
irritable, or thoughtless teacher may do much to put his
pupils in an unteachable frame of mind. Indeed, it
is no uncommon thing for a scolding or over-talkative
teacher to make his class so nervous and fretful that
steady thought with them is an impossibility. The same
may be said of an extremely nervous teacher in the class-
room. His nervousness and restlessness are imparted to
his pupils, and in either of the cases referred to here the
disorder of the class (and classes under the care of such
teachers are usually disorderly) is directly chargeable to
the teacher himself.

On the other hand, a dull, phlegmatic, easy-going
teacher is out of place in the class-room. If his pupils
do not become utterly heedless and inattentive, they will

at least take advantage of his laziness; and, again, the result will be disorder and confusion.

Executive ability shows itself nowhere to better advantage than in the class. The teacher who gives faithful attention to his class work, and at the same time successfully governs the remainder of his pupils, may be proud of his success. It needs a rare combination of qualities to be at the same time a good teacher and a successful disciplinarian.

No two teachers will conduct a recitation in precisely the same manner. No set of rules, therefore, can be given which will apply to the action of all teachers, but there are *general principles* which govern the work of class-recitation that those who expect to engage in the work of teaching would do well to heed:

1. The teacher while hearing a recitation should assume such a position as will enable him to keep all his pupils in sight.

2. In large classes it is best, when possible, for the teacher to assume a standing position; but whether sitting or standing the position should be graceful.

3. The teacher's manners in the presence of his class should be dignified and gentlemanly.

4. The teacher should be pleasant and affable in his manner of teaching, and thus control his class by his own example.

5. The teacher should so conduct his work as to keep all in the class interested and busy.

6. The teacher should show by his manner that he himself is fully interested in what he attempts to teach, and thus awaken interest on the part of his pupils.

7. The teacher's language should be well chosen and

correct, that his pupils may not lose respect for him be-cause of his many errors of speech.

8. The teacher should be enthusiastic and energetic, thus leading his pupils to feel the importance of the work in which they are engaged.

9. The teacher should use pleasant tones of voice, and thus avoid creating nervousness in either himself or his pupils.

10. The teacher should be even-tempered, not per-mitting trifles to ruffle him or provoke him to scold, and thus make his pupils disorderly.

11. The teacher should be prompt in calling and dis-missing classes, and prompt in his questions and general class work.

12. Everything in the class-recitation should be me-thodical and systematic, but not to such an extent as to destroy interest.

13. The teacher's manner should be such as to en-courage the timid and repress the impertinent.

14. The teacher should be quick to change his method of recitation the moment the interest begins to flag.

15. The teacher should take as little of the recita-tion-time as possible in reprimanding pupils. A simple shake of the head is more effective than a half hour's scolding.

16. The teacher should move about occasionally among his pupils even during recitation. This will tend to keep all orderly and busy.

17. The teacher should not be too prompt to help a pupil out of a difficulty by offering assistance. The reci-tatiou is to be made by the pupil, not the teacher.

18. The teacher should be watchful that his pupils

use correct speech in asking questions and in giving answers.

19. The teacher's manner should be such as to encourage inquiry, though he may not be able to answer all the questions asked.

20. The teacher should avoid the extreme of seeming cold, dull, phlegmatic, and uninterested, as well as the opposite of being excitable, nervous, and fretful at the weakness or tardiness of pupils.

21. The teacher should not laugh at the mistakes of his pupils, or ridicule them.

8. The Pupil in Recitation.

Pupils will differ in manner in the class-recitation as well as in their general conduct, because they differ in constitutional temperament; and the teacher must not expect pupils of a nervous, sanguine temperament to conduct themselves in the same manner as those who are dull and phlegmatic, any more than he should expect to tame a gazelle and have it work side by side with a plodding cart-horse. Pupils of different constitutional temperaments need different treatment and discipline, though the teacher should be impartial to each. The following suggestions may be made with profit to all pupils:

1. Give your full attention while in class.

2. Come to class in a teachable condition.

3. Be determined to learn all you can.

4. Do not be discouraged because you occasionally fail.

5. Be courteous and polite to your teacher and your schoolmates.

6. Do not criticise for the purpose of finding fault.

7. When you correct a mistake, do it kindly.

8. Do not laugh at the mistakes of your schoolmates.

9. Give answers in your own language.

10. Never permit a classmate to help you.

11. Never prompt a classmate to answer.

12. Speak distinctly and deliberately.

13. Rise when you answer a question, particularly if the answer be long.

14. Raise your hand when you desire to answer a question or ask for information, but do not snap the fingers to attract attention.

15. Do not speak without permission of the teacher.

16. Sit or stand erect in class. Do not lounge.

17. Pass to and from class promptly but quietly.

18. Never cheat yourself or the teacher by stealing an answer from the book or copying from your neighbor.

19. Come to the recitation always with your lesson well prepared.

20. Ask questions when you do not understand or when you desire information.

III. Examinations.

School examinations are a necessary adjunct to proper school management. They have their use, but when improperly conducted they are liable also to great abuse. As an incentive to study they are among the strongest and most effective. Unwisely managed, they may do great injustice and arouse violent opposition.

1. Objects of Examinations.

1. To Test Ability.—It is important to determine the comparative standing of .pupils and test their ability to

tell what they know. This, it may be argued, can best
he done in recitation. The pupil it must, however, be
remembered, makes special preparation for the lesson,
and under a faulty system of teaching may forget within
a month most of what he seemed to know during the
time of reciting. The examination requires him to
know and continue to know.

2. **To Act as an Incentive to Thorough Work.**—The
student who expects an examination at the close of the
month or at any other time feels, even if he have no
higher motive for study, that his knowledge must not
only be thorough, but that it must also be retained. The
examination, to him, is one of the important ends of
study, and is a powerful incentive in urging him
forward.

3. **To Secure Data.**—While the examination is not
always a true test of ability, and does not always give
reliable data upon which to classify and make promotions,
it is nevertheless, in the main, useful in connection with
the record of the pupil's class-standing during the term
as a basis on which to promote from one class to another.

4. **To Arouse Interest.**—In public schools, particularly
in rural districts, examinations are frequently found useful in creating a school sentiment among the people. The
ordinary class exercises have little in them of interest to
the patrons, but let it be known that a sharp competitive
contest is in prospect, and both their curiosity and their
interest will be at once aroused.

2. Scope of the Examination.

The ends to be attained by school examinations determine in a measure the scope and character of these tests.

1. **They should be General in Character.**—They should not deal in technicalities and minor facts. The examiner shows not only his good sense, but usually also his scholarship, in the examination. The thorough scholar, who has learned the valuable truth that the unimportant facts and details in connection with every science are almost infinite in number and variety, confines himself in his examination to questions on the general principles and most important facts, never calling for those of minor importance. He leaves these to the man who, having no comprehensive knowledge, builds his reputation on his recollection of mystic dates and figures, puzzles, and technicalities.

2. **The Examination should be Thorough.**—It should be of such a nature as to test the pupil's knowledge thoroughly as far as he has studied. The questions ought, as in the recitation, to be put in clear, definite language, that the pupil may have no difficulty in determining what his answer should be. If problems, they should be simple, but such as involve essential principles, omitting all such as require tedious and complicated work, as well as those on which authorities may be at variance.

3. **They should Test the Pupil's Power as a Thinker.**—Students frequently memorize without thinking, and in the haste of school work the teacher occasionally fails to detect the error. Questions involving the same principles taught to the pupils during the term should be given from textbooks not in the possession of those to be examined. Original questions also might be given, but still such as embrace the principles taught, and which would fairly test the pupil's familiarity with those principles and his ability to make the application.

4. Examinations should be of such a Character as to Prevent Special Preparation.—All special preparation for examination tends to foster shallow scholarship, which is worthless as soon as the examination has passed. Every examiner should discourage this special training by examining wholly on questions involving general principles. This cramming for examination defeats the most important objects of education, and dwarfs the mind instead of giving it culture.

5. Examinations should be of such a Character as to Discourage mere Memory Culture.—The question to be reached is not, Can the pupil tell what the book says on this subject? but, Does he understand the subject, and can he express his thoughts in appropriate language?—not, Can he answer all questions given in the book? but, Can he answer all questions that are based on the principles he has studied?

3. Frequency of Examinations.

The times for examinations must be regulated to some extent by the character of the school. As to the question of stated or regular time for examination, it is a debatable one. The high-pressure principle of examining all the schools of a district at the end of every month must be the device of some one whose highest idea of the business of a Superintendent is to worry pupils and send teachers to premature graves. There is no good reason why either pupils or teachers should be compelled to suffer an indignity of this kind.

The *objections* to fixed times for examinations are that some pupils will make special preparation in spite of the greatest precaution of their teachers; that they are not

usually well prepared at other times; that the anxiety
while awaiting the approaching examination often works
serious harm to both mind and body of the suffering can-
didate. Many a student has become enfeebled for life
from the dread and feverish excitement incident to an
approaching examination.

The strong argument in *favor* of unannounced examinations is that pupils must be prepared at all times, and
therefore their knowledge is more thorough than it would
be under other circumstances. Every lesson is studied
with the understanding that it may be called for at any
time, and both teacher and pupil become more thorough
in their work. The teacher ought to examine whenever
he feels that the school or the class will be benefited, but
the examinations ought not to be so frequent as to become
oppressive.

4. Method of Examining.

Examinations may be either *oral* or *written,* or both
oral and written. Each of these methods has its advocates. The method must depend somewhat on the study
in which the test is to be made.

The *oral method* in small classes has this *advantage*
over the written, that it may be made much more searching and thorough in a given time; but in large classes the
advantage in this respect is greatly in favor of the written method. The written method gives the examiner a
greater amount of work to do, and the work of examining and inspecting the papers sometimes becomes
oppressive.

A second advantage of the written method of examination is, that the same questions may be given to all the

pupils, and thus the comparative ability of the different persons examined may be more accurately determined.

In general, the written method of examination is much to be preferred to the oral, but a combination of the two is advisable, particularly when spectators are present to witness the work.

Caution.—Whatever the method pursued, the teacher should insist rigidly that there shall be no help either offered or received, and that the student who helps shall be punished quite as severely as the one who receives the help, both being guilty of wrong.

5. Length of Examinations.

The length of time occupied in an examination will depend somewhat on the ability of the teacher as an examiner. A teacher who is an expert in the work of examining will often give the candidates a fuller and fairer test with ten questions than one less skilled would with fifty.

Examinations usually are too long and tedious. Much time might be saved to both teacher and pupils by shortening them. To spend a half day in the examination of a class in a single branch is no less cruel than unwise. Examinations never should be continued so long as to tire those who are examined. When protracted to such a length that pupils become nervous and fatigued, examinations become injurious and fail as a test, because the pupils have not sufficient mental vigor to think clearly.

Suggestions.—1. Examine only on the main points; do not dwell on particulars. Prepare your questions so that they may be of a general nature.

2. Prevent special preparation for examination by giving no notice of the time. Hold your examinations at irregular intervals.

3. Let your pupils occasionally examine one another's papers; this saves work for the teacher and makes the pupils critical.

4. Do not worry your pupils by telling them constantly that they are likely to fail.

5. As the examination for promotion approaches, do not crowd your pupils and excite them. Rather train them to be cool and confident.

6. Do not classify and promote on examination percentages alone. Some of the brightest fail on examination day on account of confusion and excitement.

7. Occasionally give a short oral examination of a few minutes without any notice, that pupils may always have their knowledge at command.

8. Do not make it your chief aim to promote all the pupils in a class. Every class has its weak members.

9. Do not be in a hurry. Give your pupils plenty of time. Let them *think*, and work slowly, so that they may tell what they know.

10. Do not insist that they take up the questions in order. Let them answer those they can answer most readily first, and turn to the more difficult ones when they feel they have more time.

IV. Reviews.

The chief *objects* of reviews are the two following:

1. They Make the Pupil's Knowledge more Thorough.— Frequent reviews tend to make knowledge more thoroughly our own. The mere recalling assists us to re-member. But, in addition to this, studying with the view of having our knowledge recalled is an incentive in itself to more diligent work. Reviews are beneficial, therefore, because they assist in fixing knowledge in the mind.

2. They Test the Pupil's Knowledge.—Reviews are in a certain sense a sort of examination, and by this exam-ination the pupil's knowledge is constantly tested, the frequency of the test being measured by the frequency of the review. In some respects these review-tests are really more beneficial than a formal examination.

Frequency of Reviews.

As to the frequency and regularity of reviews, there is room for great difference of opinion. Many teachers prefer a weekly, while others advocate a monthly, re-view. There seems to be no good reason really why a slight review should not take place daily. Every day's acquisition of knowledge should be so clear in the mind of the learner that he need not fear to be questioned on the day or the week following. Unquestionably, the most valuable reviews are those which are held daily, though to these it may be well to add the weekly review, in which only the essential and most important part of the week's work should be discussed or examined.

There need be no formal method of conducting these reviews, apart from the ordinary method of questioning, though the teacher should always hold himself in readi-ness to correct any errors he may detect or answer any question that may be asked on points not fully or clearly comprehended by the pupils.

10

V. School Reports.

The following may be claimed as the chief advantages of school reports:

1. **They are Valuable as Incentives to Study and Good Conduct.**—The pupil who feels that his standing for the week or the month is to be made the basis of a report to his parents or to the school authorities is cautious to make an effort to secure the best report possible.

2. **They are Valuable in Furnishing Information.**—Parents particularly have a right to know how their children progress and how they behave while in school. Reports are valuable in furnishing this information.

3. **They are an Excellent Means of Interesting Parents in School Work.**—Few parents take so little interest in their children's success as to care nothing for their welfare and advancement. The report of a child's success or failure is a spur to the parent, and he examines the report and prizes the marked advancement quite as highly sometimes as the child himself.

The Parties to Whom Reports Should be Made.

1. **Directors or Trustees.**—By the laws of some States every teacher is compelled at the close of a school month to make his report to the Board of Directors or Trustees, through the Secretary, that these officers may have definite information relative to the school.

2. **Parents.**—This is probably the most important and beneficial report that the teacher could make. Few, however, find sufficient leisure from their school duties to make a monthly report of this character.

3. **The Newspapers.**—A conscientious report made to

the newspapers of the town in which a school is located often proves of much advantage to pupils. There are few who are not anxious to find their names among those deemed worthy of being reported to the public for advancement and correct deportment.

4. **The Superintendent.**—It would be a good plan for teachers, as an incentive to pupils, to report to the County Superintendent or School Commissioner, at the end of the month, the names of those reaching a certain standard. A record should be kept by this officer, from which occasional reports could with profit be made to the county newspapers, and the whole community might thus be kept awake to the importance of education.

These reports, which should contain a record of the pupil's attendance, deportment, and class-standing, could be made from the teacher's records.

Cautions.—1. Mark on merit alone.

2. Give earnest effort its due importance in recording the marks.

3. Mark those specially well who are original and think for themselves.

4. Mark in the student's favor rather than against him.

5. Do not be rigidly severe in marking.

6. Have no favorites when you mark.

7. Make allowance for unconscious errors.

8. Mark each branch and each topic on its own merits, not on neatness or spelling or some other hobby of your own.

9. Mark on general questions and general principles, not on technicalities or book-language.

10. Mark on a fixed standard or basis.

As to the *frequency* of marking, observe the following *cautions:*

1. Do not waste time by marking daily.

2. Do not let marking interfere with your proper work, teaching.

3. Do not use the time of the class in stopping the recitation to mark the standing of a pupil.

4. Do not mark so frequently that the pupils will strive to recite for the marks they get.

5. Mark when you are free to give it your attention, that you may not interfere with other school work.

Suggestions on School Reports.

1. Mark on some scale which can be converted to a scale having 100 representing perfection. This is the simplest and most satisfactory.

2. Pupils should not be permitted to examine the record in order to see other marks than their own, though it would be entirely proper to tell them their own marks.

3. Should a number of pupils have low marks, it is best not to show them the record, but simply explain to them that their work is not entirely satisfactory, and encourage them to do better.

4. In sending reports to parents it is thought best by many not to send the exact figures, but report simply *excellent, good, medium,* or *poor,* keeping the figures or marks for the information of the teacher alone.

5. Marking your pupils once a week will prove satisfactory generally, and it will save much labor as compared with the plan of marking daily.

6. Let the average of the pupil's work form the basis of his marks for the week.

VI. Graduation in Public Schools.

None question the importance and benefits of graduation from high schools. May not graduation from rural schools, when a specified course of study has been completed, be of equal importance, particularly as an incentive to study and regular attendance? In favor of such a plan the following arguments may be advanced:

1. Graduation from Ungraded Schools will be an Incentive to Regular Attendance.—A regular course of study having been adopted, the chance is open to every child in the district to reach that stage of progress which shall entitle him to graduation. Most pupils will appreciate the fact that the best work can be done only when they are regular in daily attendance at school.

2. Graduation Promotes Study.—The same arguments urged in the preceding paragraph might be offered in support of this proposition. The prospect of graduating is a powerful incentive to steady application and diligent study.

3. Graduation Tends to Systematize the School Work.—Pupils, feeling that they have an object to accomplish, will be more apt to enter school at the beginning of the term, their attendance will be more regular, and the school work can be performed more nearly in accordance with a fixed programme.

4. Graduation will Tend to Fix Limits to the School Work.—There is nothing at present in the school laws of the different States to prevent pupils entering school at five or six years of age and continuing up to the age of eighteen or twenty. A course of study, with graduation as the crowning feature, will, through regularity of attendance and diligent study, enable the pupils to do more between the ages of eight and sixteen years than is now done between the ages of six and twenty.

5. **Graduation will Increase the Efficiency of our Schools.** —This will be true, partly because the work will be better done in a shorter time, and partly because the public sentiment of every community will be in favor of more thorough work. Hundreds in every district will be induced to take a full course of study who under the present system care for nothing but a superficial knowledge of any of the branches.

6. **Graduation will Cause Better Teaching and More Careful Supervision.**—Every competent teacher will, under the new system, strive to compete with his associates. A beneficial rivalry will exist in every district. Such has been the case with the various ward schools in cities, and such must necessarily be the result in rural districts. The supervision of the work of teaching will also be more thorough, because better systematized and capable of producing better results.

7. **A System of Graduation will Lead to the Establishment of Township High Schools.**—Pupils who have completed the course of study in the graded schools will in general have acquired such a love for study and such a desire for more extended knowledge that they will demand something beyond the common country school. The result will be the establishment of central high schools in each township where the population is sufficiently dense to justify it, at which a higher course of study may be pursued and completed. The principal

of this school might act as General Superintendent of the other township schools, thus affording a closer supervision of them and their work than is possible under the present system, and relieving the County Superintendent or other educational officer of a part of his duties.

Examination for Graduation.—The questions for examination preparatory to graduating from the public ungraded schools should be prepared by the supervising officer ·of the county. If possible, all the examinations in a district should take place on the same day. It would be profitable to appropriate the last two Saturdays before the close of the school to this work, or where schools close at irregular times, then the two Saturdays near the time of closing the schools having the longest term.

The examining committee should consist of disinterested persons of intelligence selected by the School Board of the district or by the county superintending officer. The teacher or the members of the examining committee should then grade the papers on which the questions are answered, and their report should be submitted to the county school officer, who should attach his signature to a proper certificate or diploma to be presented to each successful applicant for examination. Following all this might come graduation day, when the pupils might celebrate the occasion by appropriate exercises, consisting of declamations, recitations, readings, essays, music, etc., for the entertainment of their friends, and then receive their diplomas as evidence that they have completed the course of study prescribed and have passed the examination with credit.

VII. A Course of Study for Country Schools.

A system of graduation necessitates a course of study to be pursued. This ought to be uniform, not only throughout the township, but also throughout the county. Indeed, if it were uniform throughout the State it would be still better. There seems to be no good reason, for instance, why each local high school in the various cities should have its own course of study. This diversity of the courses of study in the various cities makes the high-school graduate an indefinite quantity. These courses of study extend all the way from a grammar-school to a college standard, so that the title has no definite meaning. To make it have a definite significance there should be uniformity. The same is true of the course of study to be pursued in ungraded schools. It should be uniform throughout the county, and if possible throughout the State. The plan of adopting a course of study for a county is not only feasible, but it has also been found eminently practical and useful wherever the plan has been tried.

CHAPTER IV.

School Ethics.

School Ethics treats of the rights and duties of all persons connected with the school. It includes the duties of *teacher, pupils,* and *school officers.*

I. Duties of the Teacher.

The teacher's duties are not only manifold, but they are also of great importance. Taking upon himself for the parents, as he does, the responsibility of training the children under his care, he represents all the families of the community, and his duties are chiefly those which would otherwise devolve upon the parents. He has, however, duties not only to the *children* as his pupils, but also to the *parents,* to his *profession,* and to *himself.*

1. Duties to Pupils.—The duties of the teacher to pupils consist in the general nature of care-taking and providing for their wants in an *intellectual,* a *moral,* a *physical,* and an *æsthetic* sense.

1 Intellectual Wants.—Two of the chief intellectual wants of pupils are *Knowledge* and *Discipline of Mind.* These are, therefore, the wants which the teacher must be prepared to supply. It is his duty not only to communicate knowledge, but to communicate such knowledge as will be of most worth to the child as he grows to manhood, and to communicate it in such a way that the child not only may, but also that he must, understand. It is the teacher's duty also to discipline the mind of the child. He must conduct his work of instruction and recitation in such a manner as to develop the child's intellectual strength. His methods must be such as will train the child to think, ask questions, become inquisitive and anxious to learn, that it may thus be enabled to acquire mental acumen.

2. Moral Wants.—The teacher owes it to his pupils to make them good men and women. This is quite as important as to make them scholarly. It has been argued against education that it makes men rogues, but this cannot be said of the education that gives culture to the child's moral as well as his intellectual nature. An intellectual giant without a moral nature on which to base his intellectual strength, and to serve as a guide and controlling power, is an intellectual monstrosity. Such men are dangerous to the life of a nation.

Moral instruction is needed in all our schools. The methods of imparting it are many. It may be imparted in the shape of biography, holding up the example of the good and great of all times for the emulation of the children. It may be imparted by direct instruction, or in the shape of short, interesting stories, in which the moral to be taught is put in the practical shape of illustration. In whatever manner the instruction be imparted, the lesson must be made interesting and impressive; and it will serve to elevate the child's nature and prepare him for a fuller appreciation of his responsibilities as a future citizen.

Religious instruction may be imparted in a similar manner, but care must be taken that everything of a sectarian or denominational character be strictly avoided. Many an over-zealous Christian worker has defeated the whole end of both moral and religious culture by thrusting his own religious views in the face of his pupils, and thus arousing the ire of all who belonged to other sects and denominations. Where the religious views of the teacher are likely to offend or cause discord in the school work, it were better to leave them unexpressed.

3. **Physical Wants.**—The chief duty of the teacher as to the physical wants of his pupils is to see that their health is preserved, and that in their growth their intellectual tasks be of such a nature as not to interfere with healthy physical development. It is a matter of the first importance that all children of our land should have healthy physical organizations. No more pitiable sight confronts us than that of intellectual strength developed at the expense of our children's health. It is better that they should be good animals with moderate intellectual culture than that intellectual strength should be secured and health be lost for a lifetime as a result of the acquisition.

The school-house and its surroundings 'should be made conducive to health. This will require that the teacher give attention to the lighting, the heating, and the ventilation of the house; also, to the condition of the floor, the walls, the furniture, and everything else connected with the school that may by carelessness or neglect be likely to interfere with the health or the comfort of the pupils.

The personal habits of the pupils also will need the attention of the teacher. The children will need constant and oft-repeated caution with regard to their becoming overheated and attempting to cool off suddenly; also with regard to their sitting in the school-room with wet or damp clothing, sitting in drafts of air, going out of doors without proper protection from heat or cold; with regard to personal cleanliness, offensive personal habits, such as spitting on the floor, picking the teeth, and the like,—all of which ought to be avoided. They will need urging at times to induce them to take proper exercise and enough of it; and particularly will those need most urging who have the most need of exercise and the least inclination to exert themselves.

Studies should not Interfere with Health.—Care must be taken that the children's intellectual tasks be not so severe that the child's health is endangered, either by overwork or by interfering with play and exercise. These the child must have, whether he acquires intellectual culture or not. Care must be taken also that the intellectual tasks be not permitted to break down the child's nervous organization. Nothing tends more directly to this end than the constant fret and worry incident to an approaching examination, particularly when a fretful teacher adds to the annoyance by constant predictions of failure.

4. **Æsthetic Wants.**—Æsthetic culture is necessary in all schools, and possibly in no institutions is the need so intensely felt as in our American schools. From the slab-seated, plank-lined log school hut of a half century ago to the handsomely curtained and beautifully ornamented school-houses found in many districts at the present time

the distance is very great. The improvement is remark-
able, but it is only a foretaste of what we shall witness in
the future.

Æsthetic Culture Aids in Discipline.—The child who
is surrounded by beauty grows to love the beautiful and
becomes respectful. Place him in a school-room with un-
painted pine benches and desks, and he is sure to mark
them with his pencil and practice on them with his jack-
knife, and they are excellent material for the purpose.
Give him neat furniture, polished and beautified, and
he keeps both knife and pencil in his pocket. He has
an inborn love for the beautiful, and he will not mar it
unless his nature has been degraded by his associations or
by faulty teaching. Surround a child with neat school furniture and wall-decorations, such as will cultivate his taste,
and you will find that his nature will undergo a change
and he will act in harmony with his surroundings.

Æsthetic culture has been neglected, partly because we
have been too busy to give our attention to the æsthetic
nature of our children. Our commerce, our railroads,
our manufactories, our greed to make money and become
rich, have taken up our time, and the æsthetic culture of
our children has had but little attention. We need better taste, but to possess better taste our love for the beautiful must be cultivated. To cultivate a love for the
beautiful our children must be brought into the presence of
the beautiful, and both our school-rooms and our homes
must be beautified. The greed for money-getting must be
subdued for a while, and the beauty of both Art and Nature must be made to minister to the wants of our children.

2. **Duties to the Community.**—The teacher has duties

to his patrons and to the community in general. The parents of his pupils are often more deeply interested in his work and the success of their children than are the pupils themselves. His duties to his patrons include in a certain sense his duties to his pupils, and these need not here be repeated. What he owes to his pupils in the matter of culture he owes to his patrons as their parents. But he has also other duties to the community.

1. He should Interest the Community in the School Work. —To succeed well in his work the teacher must interest not only his school, but also the community in which he labors. This he can best do by interesting the children, who in turn will interest the parents in the school work. There are various ways in which this may be done, but probably none are so successful as that of suggesting some interesting question occasionally, and having the pupils ask their parents to help them in finding the answer. Any question that will set the parents to thinking will answer a good purpose. A judicious teacher can in this way set the whole community to work in search of knowledge.

2. He should Cultivate the Acquaintance of the Citizens of the Community.—The young teacher makes no more serious mistake than that of keeping aloof from the companionship of his patrons, and he can take no shorter route for destroying his influence and his usefulness. Teachers should mingle with the people of the neighborhood in which they teach. They can cultivate the acquaintance of their patrons in no better way. The teacher has duties to society which he can put aside only at the expense of his own welfare and standing. Teach_ ing as a profession would have more dignity and be more

respected if teachers felt more keenly the importance of mingling with the people of the community, and cultivating not only their acquaintance, but also their friendship.

3. **Teachers should Seek the Co-operation of their Patrons.**—Co-operation not only of the School Boards, but also of the patrons, is essential to success. The teacher should be willing to explain his plans to his patrons. Surely they are interested in the success and welfare of their children, and they will sanction and indorse plans submitted by the teacher which they would oppose and condemn if carried into execution without consultation with them. He may gain parental co-operation to some extent also by cultivating the acquaintance and friendship of his patrons, as suggested in the preceding paragraph. Encouraging citizens to visit the school will also have a good effect.

4. **He should be Frank with his Patrons.**—" Honesty is the best policy " The parent has a right to know the actual standing and progress of his child, and the teacher has no right to be untruthful about it for the purpose of either pleasing the parent or avoiding his displeasure. Right-minded parents appreciate the kindness of the teacher who gives a faithful and truthful report, though it may be an unpleasant one. The parent who inquires concerning the progress or conduct of his child usually makes the inquiry because he wants to know, and he has a right to know, the exact truth.

5. **He should Cultivate a School Sentiment in the Community.**—This should be done in a modest way. He should remember that though his patrons, as a rule, may not be so well educated as himself, their experience in

life may be quite as valuable to them as his book-learning is to him. Many of these patrons are persons of sound judgment, and they will appreciate modest worth and merit without having their attention specially directed to it. The modest teacher who anxiously and earnestly does the best he can to create an educational sentiment in the community will usually succeed. The teacher should consult with the prominent citizens, invite them to his school-room, seek their advice and aid, and through them interest the community.

3. **Duties to his Profession.**—*Teaching is a profession.* The Creater has endowed man with various mental powers or faculties. These need training and culture, that man may be properly developed, and that he may acquire the full stature of perfect manhood, and thus fill the place designed for him. To cultivate these faculties is the work of the teacher, and it is a work requiring not only as great learning for its proper performance, but also as much skill, as that of either law, medicine, or theology. Surely, there is no calling in life which has a nobler work, nor any which requires a more intricate knowledge of man's mental and physical organization. It is true, many assume to teach who have neither the requisite skill nor the requisite learning to do this work properly. But no profession is without its quacks and failures. Not every man that wields the scalpel is a successful surgeon, nor every one that enters the pulpit a successful preacher. Neither is every one that pleads before the court a successful practitioner at the bar. It would be unfair, therefore, to expect all teachers to rise to the dignity of professors until all have the proper

preparatory training and scholarship to fit them for the full and faithful performance of their duty.

The teacher has certain duties to his profession. The chief of these are—

1. **He should Dignify it by his Scholarship.**—No one needs thorough scholarship so much as does the teacher. Mere learning which lies in the mind like so much dry lumber stored in an attic will not suffice; it must be knowledge which the possessor can recall and use as occasion demands; it must be a weapon which he can wield with effect. His scholarship must be liberal, embracing a knowledge of much outside of his special work; but as to all incident to his profession his knowledge should not only be comprehensive, but also that of a specialist. There should be nothing in connection with his calling which he should not at least strive to know. Much of this knowledge he must gain by close observation and by experience in the school-room, but this effort at self-culture will make his knowledge all the more reliable, because it makes him a thinker.

2. **The Teacher should Dignify his Profession by his Personal Character.**—The men who engage in teaching should be men whose personal character is worthy of imitation. Not only should they be upright in conduct, but also in speech. The principles they attempt to instill should be above question. No man whose teachings cannot be strictly followed, or whose character and habits cannot be profitably imitated, should be permitted to enter the school-room as a teacher.

3. **The Teacher should Avoid being Dogmatic.**—Dealing with the child-mind as the teacher does, no one is in greater danger than he of putting too high an estimate

on his own ability, and of asserting his opinion in such a manner as to assume that it *must* be correct because he says it. Teachers must avoid becoming opinionated if they hope to have their profession respected. Great care must be taken that they do not become egotistic, and thus bring disgrace and disrepute on their calling.

4. The Teacher should Show Respect to his Fellow-Teachers.—The interests of the profession demand this. Every other profession is characterized by an *esprit de corps* which lends dignity to that profession. Teachers, possibly the quacks only, are too often willing that their profession shall be made the subject of all kinds of witless and silly jokes and disrespectful remarks. All other professions defend the dignity and magnify the importance of their work, and it is left for teachers alone to hear their calling ridiculed and denounced without defending it and themselves. Self-respect will make us respect one another. All jealousy or envy at others' success must be subdued. No one needs sympathy more than does the teacher, and from no one ought he to expect sympathy more than from his fellow-teacher. The interests both of the individual and the profession, therefore, demand that there shall be a spirit of fellowship and kindness among the members of that calling.

5. The Teacher should Seek to Elevate his Calling.—This may be done in various ways. Prominent among the means of professional improvement are—

a. Normal Schools.—The object of these schools is the preparation of teachers for their profession. They bear the same relation to teaching as the various professional schools bear to the other learned professions. They do not always make successful teachers and disciplinarians, any more than do medical colleges always make successful surgeons and physicians, or other professional schools make adepts in the professions they teach; but they nevertheless do a grand work in teaching the principles which underlie the whole work of instruction and discipline. They have not the power to reconstruct human organization or reverse Nature, and therefore cannot make teachers of men and women whose temperaments and general mental characteristics do not fit them for this profession; and yet they can help even these. So important is the work they do and so fully are their merits and efficiency appreciated that they have become recognized as government institutions in nearly all the most progressive states and nations of the world.

b. Teachers' Institutes.—These, in a measure, do similar work to that of the normal schools, but being convened for only a short time, and being usually unclassified, the work must necessarily be of a more general character. Much professional improvement may be gained from the association of teachers in this manner, but more important than this is the professional feeling which is engendered and the *esprit de corps* which is established. The comparison of views and methods, the mutual consultation, and the enthusiasm awakened, are most beneficial, not only to the teachers, but ultimately to the schools also over which they preside. They give to young teachers a higher estimate of the importance and magnitude of the work in which they are engaged.

c. Teachers' Libraries.—The teacher who does not read at least some works on the profession in which he is engaged is merely a quack. Teachers ought to keep pace with the times. The non-progressive teacher constantly retrogrades, because progress is onward. The methods of teaching and management to-day differ very greatly from the methods and management of twenty-five years ago. The teacher, therefore, who does not keep pace with the times by reading educational works and educational journals does more toward degrading than toward elevating his profession. There is no teacher, not even the most learned or the most progressive, who may not learn something from the educational journals of the day.

d. School Visitation.—Professional information may be gained also by visiting the schools of others. It would be economical for every School Board to give to each of its teachers a half day every month for the purpose of visiting other schools. No two teachers perform their work in the same manner. Visitation would enable a teacher not only to observe what is good in others' teaching, but also to correct his own errors by witnessing the errors of others. Faithful teachers are always anxious to improve, and they find school visitation in every way profitable.

e. Writing for the Press.—Other professions as well as teaching have their journals, and the members of those professions find it greatly to their advantage not only to read these journals, but also to communicate their ideas through them to the public. It would greatly aid in elevating teaching to its proper place if all that originate successful plans or try successful experiments would cause them to be known to their fellow-teachers through the columns of educational newspapers. It is the duty of successful teachers to write for the press, and lend every effort to elevate their profession to its proper rank.

4. Duties to Himself.—The two chief duties which the teacher owes to himself are *The Care of his Health* and *Self-Culture.*

1. **The Teacher's Care of his Health.**—Few employments are so exhaustive to both mind and body as is teaching, and there are few callings in which good health is so necessary. The nature of the work, combined with the fact that the teacher is confined to the one room during the day, without sunshine and sometimes in the foulest of atmospheres, has certainly much to do with undermining the teacher's health. If his personal habits conform to the requirements of hygienic laws, and he preserve a cheerful temper, there is little reason why any teacher should be afflicted with ill health as the result of his work in the school-room. Worry wears faster than work. Let the teacher, therefore, preserve an even temper and conform strictly to the laws by which health is preserved, and he will have little cause to complain of the arduous duties of the school-room. Exercise, food, sleep, air, bathing, and dress will all need proper attention.

2. **Self-Culture.**—The teacher should strive diligently to improve himself. The nature of his work demands that his mind be constantly on the alert. He is the example which his pupils will imitate, and for their sake, as well as his own, his thoughts must be fresh and his mind constantly supplied with the riches drawn from Nature's storehouse of knowledge. It is often said that young teachers are frequently the best; because they are enthusiastic and anxious to learn, while those who remain in the profession for a great length of time become in a measure careless and indifferent. This may be true, but certainly it ought not to be so. Every teacher ought to

feel that he has a duty to himself in the matter of self-culture and self-improvement, and that he must be progressive as a matter of self-interest.

II. Duties of Pupils.

The chief duties of pupils are—

1. **Duties to Themselves.**—These consist mainly of study for the sake of improvement, care of their school property, such as books, pencils, etc., care of their clothing, and care of their persons in such manner as to preserve health.

2. **Duties to One Another.**—These consist in the respect which they owe to the rights of others. They owe it to their schoolmates to avoid all injury to either their persons or their property.

3. **Duties to the Teacher.**—It is the duty of pupils to be attentive, respectful, and obedient. The teacher's property also must not be interfered with by pupils. They should also have regard for his personal comfort.

4. **Duties to School Officers.**—Pupils owe respect to the officers who have charge of the schools. It is their duty also to refrain from injuring the school property placed in the care of these officers.

5. **Duties to Visitors.**—These consist mainly in showing them respect and courtesy, and seeing that they are made comfortable during their visits to the school.

6. **Duties to the Community.**—Pupils should avoid interfering with the comfort of those living near the school by refraining from excessive noise. They should not trespass upon the grounds or property of the neighbors, and should refrain from being impolite or disrespectful.

III. Duties of School Officers.

The chief school officers who come in contact with both the teacher and the pupils are known variously in different states as School Directors, School Trustees, and Committee-men. Want of space will prevent a full discussion of their duties here, hence we do but little more than indicate them.

1. They should Select Proper School Sites.—This they owe to the health and comfort of the children, whose character is to some extent moulded by the school surroundings.

2. They should Build Comfortable and Beautiful School-houses.—These, too, have their influence in forming character, and while comfort should have due consideration, beauty must not be neglected. Beautiful school-houses tend to create higher ideals and promote nobility of character.

3. They should Adopt Proper Textbooks.—It is a puzzling question sometimes among many excellent text-books to know what to adopt, but school officers will find the opinion of disinterested successful teachers always the safest to follow. When good textbooks, adapted to the wants of the pupils are to be had, it is little less than criminal to keep inferior ones in use for the reason that a change may cause some expense to the district. No mechanic uses worn-out and worthless machinery when he can purchase new which will do his work better and more satisfactorily.

4. They should Adopt Grades of Study.—A course of study should be adopted, not only by the school officers of towns and cities, but also by those of rural districts.

System will do much toward improving the school. A course of study not only for a district, but for a whole county, is advisable.

5. They should Employ Competent Teachers.—The teachers should be well qualified in every sense, physi cally, intellectually, morally, and professionally. School officers should secure the best teaching possible. If the salaries they offer will not command the proper talent and qualifications, there is only one remedy, and that is to pay better salaries. Low salaries will always fill the positions with incompetent and unworthy applicants.

6. They should Supervise and Visit the Schools.— School officers are the representatives of the people, and it becomes their duty to see that the school work is done in the best possible manner. They should visit the schools frequently, both for the purpose of witnessing the teacher's work and for the purpose of giving teacher and pupils encouragement. They should have the teacher feel that their visits are friendly calls made for the purpose of cheering and encouraging, not for faultfinding. No man is so unfit to be a Director or Trustee as one who feels it his duty to grumble and find fault.

7. They should Encourage Educational Sentiment in the Community.—No persons have greater power than school officers to arouse an educational interest in the community. If they indorse the teacher and his methods, the people are satisfied that the work is properly done. School officers should not only co-operate with the teacher, but also secure the co-operation of the patrons, and thus establish such entire harmony as cannot fail to result in good to all.

IV. Duties of the Superintendent.

The chief duties to be performed by the Supeiintend-ent or School Commissioner are specified by law, and they need not be mentioned here. Independent of these are other duties which the welfare of the schools demand of this officer.

1. He should Seek to Elevate Teaching to its Proper Rank as a Profession.—This he can do in various ways, but especially by granting certificates to competent teachers only. The standard of qualifications should be advanced from year to year, and the day hastened when all certificates shall be of the first grade and strictly professional. No other profession grades the standing of its members, and there seems to be no good reason why teachers should be graded in this manner. Ability and success should in teaching determine the professional standing, as they do in other professions.

2. He should Harmonize School Interests.—The Super-intendent ought to see that harmony prevails between the Directors and the teachers, and between the teacher and the patrons. A judicious Superintendent can do much toward promoting harmony among the various school-workers, and thus add greatly to the welfare of the schools. The school work of the county should be well systematized, and the teachers and the Directors be made to feel that all are working for the same purpose and to the same end.

3. He should Create a Public Sentiment in Favor of Good Schools.—This he can do by holding educational meetings in the various school districts, at which educational addresses may be made, and in which also the pu-

pils of the various schools of the district may be brought together and unite in exercises of interest to both themselves and their parents. An energetic Superintendent is capable of doing great good by arousing the patrons of a district with meetings of this kind, and making them enthusiastic in the cause of good schools.

4. He should Encourage Good Teaching.—The business of the Superintendent is not faultfinding. He should rather encourage. Where it is necessary to find fault he should do so kindly, privately pointing out the errors to the teacher, and showing at the same time how they may be corrected. Where he finds good work done he should give proper commendation, and when an opportunity occurs to speak favorably of good teachers he should never hesitate to do so. Such a course of conduct on the part of a Superintendent will be beneficial not only to the weak teachers by assisting them to be strong, but it will also make the strong stronger.

CHAPTER V

School Government.

Government is the administration of laws for the purpose of preserving order. School government is the administration of school affairs in such a manner as to secure proper discipline and promote the greatest welfare of the school. It does not differ materially from family government. Its end is the same, that of making good citizens. Family government is a union properly of divine and civil government. This is true also of school government. The teacher takes the place of the parent, and assumes for the time all the rights and responsibilities of that person. School government is, however, much the more difficult of the two, because it represents an aggregation of families, each with its own system, and in many of which government is extremely defective.

1. Objects of School Government.

Among the objects of school government the following are the most important:

1. To Preserve Order.—Order is necessary, that school work may be performed to the best advantage, but order does not necessarily mean absolute quiet. Quiet may be secured by the enforcement of rigid penalties, but it is a kind of quiet which is detrimental to the best interests of the school. The machinery of the school-room when in good working condition is quite as likely to produce

171

some noise as the machinery in well-regulated manufactories; hut-a degree of quiet and regularity sufficient to permit the school work to go on without interruption must be observed at all times. One of the chief objects of school government is to secure this order and regularity.

2. To Train to Self-Government.—Probably the most important object of school government is that of training pupils to govern and control themselves. The children in our schools represent the different varieties of family government in the community, and the teacher who can harmonize all these, selecting the strong points and discarding the weak, performs a task the magnitude of which cannot be over-estimated.

The power to govern well, to train pupils to self-control, to lift up the weak and fill them with self-respect, to curb the wayward and lead them to the performance of their duty, is the essential characteristic of every successful teacher. Without this ability it is unwise for any one to engage in the work of teaching.

Children are creatures of impulse. Many of them, while not vicious, are heedless and thoughtless. Others are not only heedless, but also merciless and tyrannical, and they like nothing better than a contest with the new teacher. Let him in this preliminary skirmish win the day, and it is won for all time, but if he lose it he need hope for little comfort in his efforts to manage that school in the future.

With those pupils whose impulses are strong, and whose moral powers are yet uncultured and untrained, self-control is necessarily weak. Control of self is the first lesson they have to learn, and it is also in many respects the most important. The wise instruction of both the teacher and the parent is necessary to teach it. Nor can the lesson be learned in a few months. A school life is too short to teach it thoroughly. The teacher must not therefore be discouraged at seeming failure.

2. School Control.

The three chief officers to whom all school control is delegated are the Teacher, the Directors or Trustees, and the County Commissioner or Superintendent. The local Trustees in some States are equivalent to the township Directors in other States, and the office of County Superintendent in some is similar in a measure to that of County School Commissioner in others.

Of these officers, the teacher comes in closest relations to the pupils, though the authority of all extend over the schools, and each office has its separate duties and responsibilities; and it is these duties and responsibilities which give to us a system of School Ethics in which are included the duties of teacher, pupils, and school officers.

3. Elements of Governing Power.

To be a good disciplinarian requires certain characteristics in the teacher which are called for in no other vocation or profession. His field for work is wider and his responsibilities are greater than those of any other calling. He represents all the families of the community with all their diverse systems of government, and his discipline must be such as not only wins absolute success for him in the school-room, but also secures for him the indorsement and approbation of his patrons and school officers.

The chief of these *characteristics* are—

1. System.—To govern well, the teacher must be systematic in all he does. He should not only have his pupils work according to a fixed programme, but he himself should have his day's work mapped out and provided for before he opens school in the morning. Every movement of his pupils and every recitation should be conducted in a systematic manner. He should be prompt in all he does, and thus be systematic as to time. He should see that everything is in its proper place, and thus be systematic and orderly as to place. Nothing so detracts from good discipline as the carelessness of a slovenly teacher.

Orderly habits are to be commended, not only in the teacher, but also in the pupils. Orderly habits established in the school-room become orderly habits for life. The teacher should therefore encourage his pupils to be neat and orderly in their dress, in the care of their books, their desks, and the school furniture in general.

2. Energy.—An industrious, energetic teacher finds little difficulty in managing his pupils and keeping them busy, which, after all, is one of the secrets of good discipline. The busy child is rarely troublesome or mischievous. It is the idler that finds time to annoy his schoolmates and the teachers with his mischief. Energy in the teacher makes the pupils energetic, and overcomes obstacles and difficulties which seem almost insurmountable. Energy is work, and work is genius.

3. Vigilance.—The successful disciplinarian is watchful without being a spy. Constant watchfulness is necessary to preserve order and to detect the coming storms. All

mischief and disorder is much more readily prevented than corrected. It is best, therefore, to prevent mischief rather than wait for it to occur, and then punish a child for what the teacher might and should have prevented.

The Teacher should not be a Spy.—No persons are more unfit to govern than they who show constant suspicion and distrust of their pupils. The spying teacher usually finds all the disorder, confusion and trickery that he is in search of, but in playing the spy he shows himself unworthy of his office. The teacher can be watchful and alive to all that is going on without playing the part of detective. He should of course not close his eyes to wrong-doing, but at the same time he should not magnify small offenses and imagine them aimed at the good order of the school.

The Vigilant Teacher should Encourage.—His mission is not faultfinding. Many trivial offenses and faults are overlooked because to call attention to them would give them an air of importance which they do not deserve. It is best to encourage and praise where it is possible to do so, and find fault or censure only where the offense is of such a character or has been so frequently repeated as to interfere with the welfare of the school.

4. Self-Control.—The man who hopes to teach his pupils self-control must first be certain that he is able to control himself. Self-control gives the teacher that quiet dignity which is a necessity in order to secure and retain the respect of the pupils. It gives him also that self-possession which enables him to decide on all difficulties with promptness and certainty. It enables him to keep his powers ready and quick to respond at call.

The Teacher should Avoid showing Anger.—The teacher whose temper becomes his master soon loses control of his pupils. Though at first his exhibition of anger may frighten the children, the frequent repetition of these fits of anger makes him ridiculous, and he loses the children's respect and love. Anger is justifiable only when the pupil has attempted to interfere deliberately and maliciously with the welfare of the school by committing some serious offense.

The Teacher should be Patient.—Many things will occur to vex and irritate him, and particularly is this likely to be true when his nerves are unstrung by ill health or overwork. But it is his duty to be patient even under these trying circumstances. Children learn slowly; they are forgetful, and they thoughtlessly commit offenses against which they have been warned again and again. Through all these trials the teacher must be patient, and thus will he win the respect and love of even the most thoughtless and wayward.

The Teacher should be Cheerful.—The cheerful teacher succeeds best in his discipline. The man who can thwart mischief by turning the joke on the perpetrator rarely fails in discipline. The cheerful teacher is a power in the school-room, and his influence is tenfold more potent in securing proper discipline than all the rules and regulations that can be enacted. He scatters joy and sunshine where his grumbling neighbor distributes grief and shadows; and his pupils leave him at the end of their school career showering blessings on him and feeling grateful for the work he has accomplished in making them worthy men and women.

The Teacher should Avoid Controversy with his Pupils.

—Antagonism between teacher and pupils lowers each in the estimation of the other. Under no circumstances should the teacher so far forget himself as to quarrel or argue with a pupil in ill-humor. Nor should the teacher under any circumstances permit pupils to reply to him in an insolent or impertinent manner. Discipline must be preserved at all hazards—by pleasant, cheerful communication with pupils if this be possible, but if not by this means, then by letting the pupil understand that obedience to law is the first requisite.

5. **Confidence.**—The teacher who hopes to succeed must have confidence—

In his Work.—The man who does not believe in the nobleness of the teacher's work has no business in the school-room. Those who regard teaching as a mere stepping-stone by which to rise to other positions, and to be occupied only until some calling more remunerative claims their attention, are not teachers in the proper sense of the term, nor do they ever succeed as does he who devotes his whole energy to the work, and who has full faith that he is engaged in a calling inferior in no respect to any other which engages the attention and talents of his fellow-men.

In his Pupils.—In no way can the teacher secure better discipline and more earnest hard work than by showing his pupils that he has entire confidence in them and their intention to do right. At no time should he permit them to believe that he thinks them unworthy of his confidence. It is the first step toward their ruin. Let him trust his pupils, and they will show themselves worthy of being trusted. Even the hardened criminal

12

is elevated by showing him that you have faith in his honesty.

In Himself.—The teacher must have confidence not only in his work, but also in himself. He must feel that he is competent to perform the work which is placed before him. He need not and should not be egotistic, for this will greatly interfere with his success, but he should know how to esteem and measure his own ability. His scholarship should be such that he feels entire confidence in his ability to teach all that may be required of him. His knowledge of management and methods must be such as to make him feel that he is entirely competent to perform the work of governing and teaching to the satisfaction of both the school and the community. He should have a due estimate of himself, and yet with it all he must be modest and not inclined to dogmatism.

6. Culture.—Culture of mind, manners, and voice are great aids in discipline.

Culture of Mind.—This includes not only scholarship, but also the ability to grapple firmly with difficulties in study, and dispose of them promptly as they arise in the daily school work. A well-disciplined mind, though not equal, possibly, in scholarship to another undisciplined and improperly cultured, will much more readily adapt means to ends, and much more readily apply principles in such a way as to win at once the esteem and confidence of pupils.

Culture of Manners.—Pupils imitate their teachers. A polished lady or gentleman in the teacher's chair will in time produce ladylike and gentlemanly pupils. The boorish teacher, with unpolished boots and soiled clothes, will also have his imitators and followers. It is of the greatest possible importance that the teacher be a model in his deportment and personal habits. Let him sit in an awkward position, his pupils will imitate; let him be addicted to offensive personal habits, his pupils will quote him as an example; let him, on the other hand, be polished and polite, lifting his hat to his pupils as he meets them, the manners of the whole community will change and he will find himself an object of respect.

Culture of Voice.—Culture of voice is also an important factor in discipline. The teacher should cultivate pleasant tones of voice. In no case should he speak harshly, or louder than is necessary for his pupils to hear him distinctly. The teacher often makes his school noisy by being himself noisy in manner and voice. He should not talk too much. Discipline is gained often quite as effectually by allowing the pupils to talk in recitation while the teacher listens. The scolding and faultfinding tone of voice is too prevalent in our school-rooms, even at the present day, to be productive of good order.

7. **Love.**—Love is a ruling principle of discipline. The ability to make our pupils not only respect us for our personal worth, but at the same time love us because of our interest in their welfare and our kindness toward them, is one that every teacher should possess. To command this love and respect argues certain qualities in the teacher which aid him greatly in discipline.

He should Love his Pupils.—The teacher who loves his pupils manifests that love in his desire to benefit them. He is kind and considerate. Feeling that he is interested in their welfare, the pupils learn to love

, and the work of discipline is very greatly

l Try to Make his Pupils Happy.—The faithful teacher adds daily to the happiness of those in his care. Sometimes he does it by offering a word of encouragement, sometimes by sympathizing with them, sometimes by soothing, sometimes by adding to their personal comfort, but through it all showing the loving heart which dictates all this kindness.

Obedience is Won by Love.—The pupils placed under a loving teacher, whose guidance they soon learn to estimate at its highest worth, obey cheerfully because love dictates cheerful obedience. The teacher is found to be a loving friend rather than an arrogant despot, and obedience becomes a pleasure. Indeed, it is not in the nature of things to do otherwise than respect and obey those whom we love.

8. **Personal Magnetism.**—There are men and women who seem to have been born to influence and control their fellows. What the latent element in their character is which gives them this control and influence it is difficult to say. For want of a better name, it is usually denominated personal magnetism. It is the power which brings to a man friends and surrounds him with associates, though he may have neither wealth nor position to bestow. It is the power which enables many a man to say commonplace things in a commonplace way, and yet often please an audience far better than could the profoundest wisdom of the most revered sages and philosophers.

The teacher who is possessed of this magnetic character

need have little fear of failure in discipline. His school will in a great measure control and regulate itself. Pupils will do right and strive to please him because they find a pleasure in doing so. Patrons will sustain him because they find their children pleased and ready to defend the teacher. It is this same power that gave unlimited success to Pestalozzi, Arnold, Page, and others who have proved themselves the great teachers of the world.

9. Executive Power.—Closely allied to personal governing power is that talent which many possess of wisely adapting means to ends, and thus winning for themselves the power to govern. Many elements enter into this power. The basis of all, however, is good judgment, or what is usually known as good common sense.

There are those in every community toward whom people turn for advice. They are men whose judgment in a measure regulates the thought and action of that community. These persons are born managers, and they succeed in every calling in life in which sound judgment is one of the requisites. We all feel that we can rely on the counsel of a man whose judgment is cool and deliberate and whose action is well considered. Such men are natural leaders, and in the history of the world they have always asserted their power.

Judgment may be Trained.—Common sense may be inborn, but there is no question that that faculty of mind which we know as "judgment" may be cultured, and thus acquire greater executive power. This culture needs coolness and deliberation on our part. It needs the subduing of temper and personal choice to some extent. It needs at times the subordination of our own will to that of others. It needs at times a temporary defeat, that we may gain a final victory. It needs that we sometimes seem to follow, while in reality we guide and direct.

Wise School Government seeks Co-operation.—The teacher who undertakes to conduct his school independent of the wishes and opinions of the community meets not only with opposition, but often with utter failure. The wise teacher seeks the co-operation not only of his patrons, but also of his Directors or Trustees. He does not say decidedly, "I shall do this," or, "I shall do that," but rather, "Had I not better do this?" or, "Had I not better do that?" He leads by seeming to follow. He meets the objector on the threshold, takes him by the hand, welcomes him cordially to the school-room, interests him in the exercises, consults him on a point or two about the whole school, and particularly about his own child, explains to him the school plans, parts with him at the close of the school day as a warm friend, and sends him out into the community on a mission to convert others. This is tact, executive talent, good judgment, wise management.

10. **Will-Power.**—Strength of will in the teacher is essential to good government. The child must be made to feel that law is necessary, and that the teacher is the ruling power in the school-room. He must be made to feel also that his own will must be curbed, and where the interest of the school demands it be made to harmonize with that of others. The teacher's will must of course be supreme. He is the ruler, and if he be possessed of the proper executive power and tact he will have little difficulty in guiding and directing his pupils.

The Teacher's Will must be Firm.—A vacillating policy

is always weak. The teacher who at first refuses, then relents, and at last consents, shows a weakness of will-power which is not conducive to good government. But the teacher who finds himself in error should never be so cowardly as to fear making acknowledgment of his mistake. It is a grave error to think that we ought never to reverse our judgment. Indeed, it is a plain duty to correct ourselves when in error, that our pupils may not fall into the same mistakes.

Firmness and Kindness must be United.—The teacher who depends wholly on his will-power and his firmness is not well prepared to draw his pupils to him and control them by appeals to their better nature. He may rule with a rod of iron, and thus secure order and quiet, but it is a sort of rule which awakens no kindly sympathy between teacher and pupils, and which in the end must be productive of discord and friction the moment the iron grasp is relaxed. Let kindness be associated with firmness; let pupils feel that the teacher is their friend, and that whatever seeming arbitrary power he may exercise is exerted for their welfare as individuals and for the welfare of the school, and obedience will be recognized as a duty. Pupils will obey such discipline cheerfully where they chafe and fret under the iron rule of will-power alone, or become reckless, uninterested, and listless under the government of one whose will-power is weak.

11. The Teacher must have Power to Punish.—Human nature has not yet reached that approximate perfection which will permit us to govern without punishment. There are stubborn natures which at times can be

no other way. It is idling time to argue
be governed by moral suasion and by appeals
A teacher who possesses all the elements of
here named will succeed in nearly every case
without resort to punishment, and yet so long as human
nature is imperfect we shall find some children in our
schools who must be governed by a firm hand, and who
can be reached at times only by inflicting punishment.

It is a mistake for school officers to deprive the teacher
of the power to punish. The teacher's influence is thus
weakened, and the insolence of evil-minded children is
capable not only of making his position unpleasant, but
also of rendering him incapable of accomplishing good.
It is wiser to give the teacher the power to punish, and hold
him responsible for the abuse of that power in punishing
too frequently or too severely.

12. Teaching-Power.—One of the most important elements of good discipline is teaching-power. The ability
to arouse one's pupils, to interest them, and set them
to thinking for themselves, is a rare gift. Hearing
recitations is not teaching. Keeping good order in
school is not teaching. Teaching-power consists in the
ability to make your pupils feel the importance of the
work in which they are engaged, arouse their enthusiasm,
and create a love for learning. Its results are scholarship
and culture, not the ability only to state facts as recorded
in books without comprehending them.

Teaching-Power Creates Interest.—The power to teach
well means also the power to govern well. All things
else being equal, the teacher who can interest his pupils
rarely finds them inclined to do mischief or create dis-

order. The interesting teacher directs the energies of his pupils into proper channels, and thus secures work instead of mischief. The pupils, who catch the enthusiasm of their teacher and follow his lead, rarely find time for mischief, and when engaged in work the school becomes largely self-governing and self-regulating. It is a doubtful policy, however, to permit one's self to become so enthusiastic as to forget that quiet and order are essential to study. The teacher who permits his enthusiasm or that of his pupils to become so boisterous as to interfere with the study of those not engaged in recitation does quite as much harm as he who fails to govern because of other incompetence.

13. Impartiality.—The teacher acts not only as a legislator, framing the laws for his school, but also as a judge. In this capacity he must be strictly impartial, dealing fairly and justly with every pupil. He will of course love some better than others, for the simple reason that some are more lovable and more worthy of love than others; but this must not interfere with his government. So far as his school laws and discipline are concerned, he must have no favorites. All should enjoy the same privileges and receive the same impartial treatment. Every decision he renders should be weighed in the scales of exact justice to all. Judgments thus rendered will serve to win for him the love and respect of his pupils, and good discipline will be secured.

4. Causes of Disorder.

Independent of the restless activity of child-nature, which often leads to disorder in school, there are causes which produce disturbance and discord for which the pupils are not directly responsible, and for which it would be manifestly improper to punish them. The wise plan is to remove these causes of disorder, and with them the temptation to do wrong. The following are among the chief:

1. **Improper Ventilation.**—There are few teachers who have not learned the value of pure air in maintaining good discipline as well as in securing effective study. Students compelled to breathe impure air become restless, and find it difficult to confine themselves to work except under forced pressure. The teacher also finds himself inclined to become irritable, and he gives attention to trifling interruptions and seeming offenses which at other times would not claim a thought. The school is a good barometer, showing the approaching storm by the restless condition of both pupils and teacher.

2. **Uncomfortable School-Houses.**—School-houses improperly heated, as well as those improperly ventilated, are conducive to disorder. Pupils who are suffering with extreme heat or extreme cold find it a matter of great difficulty to forget their bodily discomfort and fix their attention closely on their study. Students under such circumstances must become restless and disorderly. It is a natural result of their bodily suffering. The evil is beyond the reach of both pupils and teacher, and it can be remedied only by the Board of Directors or Trustees.

3. **Uncomfortable Seatings.**—These have also much to do with disorder in the school-room. Hard benches, with straight backs ill adapted to the natural curvature of the body, and so high that a child's feet cannot rest comfortably on the floor, tend to tire the pupils and make

them shift position frequently in order to be comfortable. High desks have the same effect, and this desire to be comfortable, and the consequent frequent changing of position in a school of fifty or more pupils, must necessarily produce noise and consequent disorder.

4. **Ill-Health of Pupils.**—The ill-health of pupils is a frequent cause of restlessness. Defective ventilation and excessive worry are both liable to cause headache, and this in turn unfits the pupil either for effective study or for preserving good order. Schools are frequently annoyed also by the almost incessant coughing of such pupils as carelessly expose themselves to drafts of air, or who overheat themselves and cool too suddenly, thus contracting colds.

5. **Nervousness.**—Nervousness of both pupils and teacher, or of either, is apt to produce more or less disorder in the school-room. The nervous teacher is apt to become unnecessarily agitated, and thus cause nervousness and excitement among the pupils. But nervous pupils are apt to become restless under the most even-tempered teacher.

6. **Contagious Laughter.**—Nothing is so vexatious as the disposition which pupils occasionally manifest to giggle and laugh without any apparent cause. This laughter, too, becomes contagious, and the trouble thus begun is likely to continue indefinitely. Scolding on the part of the teacher either makes it worse or changes the laughter to anger. It would be entirely proper to dismiss a pupil from class if he persist in amusing himself and disturbing others in this manner. Some teachers cure this disposition to laugh foolishly by setting apart a few minutes when the laugh is most likely to come, and devote it to a laughing exercise in which only the laughers shall

participate. It is a severe cure, but it is usually an effective one.

7. Whispering.—This is one of the puzzling questions
of school-management. Pupils will whisper, just as grown
folks will talk, when they find companions with whom
they may carry on a conversation. Whispering is a cause
of disorder, and it is sometimes annoying to both studi
ous pupils and the teacher. What shall we do about it?
Shall we enact strict rules that there shall be no whispering on penalty of punishment? Few teachers have found
such rules effective, and fewer still have found them less
annoying to the teacher than to the pupil. An inflexible
rule which visits punishment upon every offending one
that whispers makes no distinction between the vicious
and the thoughtless, and is therefore unjust.

Whispering is best subdued by requests. Rigid rules
only make the children deceitful, and train them to sub-
stitute deaf-mute alphabet signs or note-writing for whispering, either of which takes more time and is more annoying than the whispering itself. Pupils should not be
left to understand that they dare whisper whenever they
please, but instead that whispering is discountenanced,
that it interferes with study, that it annoys the teacher
and the pupils, that it wastes valuable time, etc. If pupils are at first unable to control their desire to whisper,
the teacher might with profit give a whispering recess of
a minute or so every hour, which would serve as an escape-
valve. Pupils will appreciate the kindness, and then
devote their time during the study-period entirely to
study. An over-rigid adherence to rule quite as often
causes mischief as does the whispering itself. Pupils
have a natural desire to talk and ask questions. It is

best to control and regulate that desire, rather than curb it. The teacher is not wiser than Nature, and he must not take it for granted that Nature is all wrong and that she must be corrected.

Few teachers ever succeed fully in breaking up the habit of whispering. There is more important school work demanding the attention of teachers than the constant watchfulness for culprits. Let the teacher wisely guide and direct the efforts of Nature, and success is always within reach ; and this is the proper remedy for whispering, as well as for all other school faults.

8. A Disorderly Teacher.—The teacher's personal con duct has much to do with the good order of his school. Pupils are imitative. A bright, cheerful teacher has bright, cheerful pupils, while one who is fretful will annoy his pupils and worry them into fretfulness. A noisy, disorderly teacher always has a noisy and disorderly school. The maxim is old, but always true: "As is the teacher, so is the school." The teacher therefore must be orderly, that he may secure order. His manner of address to the pupils must be pleasant and conversational ; his manner of walking across the floor must be such as not to attract attention. If he speak in loud tones, his pupils will speak in loud tones, and if his movements about the room be noisy, he will find ready imitators among the children.

9. A Timid Teacher.—Pupils soon learn to appreciate force of character, and they never fail to lose their respect for a teacher who is so timid as to fear his pupils. Let the pupils once discover that the teacher is afraid to maintain his authority, and that authority is gone. We often respect men because they respect themselves, but

the over-meek man, whose timidity frightens him into absolute humility, wins the respect of neither men nor children.

10. A Suspicious Teacher.—Possibly no teacher provokes pupils to commit deeds of disorder more than one who is constantly on the watch for mischief. Students like to measure their ability to play tricks and escape the detection of a teacher who is on the constant lookout for evil. A suspicious teacher always finds himself in trouble, for the simple reason that no one feels like committing mischief half so much at any time as when he knows that he is suspected of wrong-doing. To win a victory over a teacher who prides himself on keeping good order because he is constantly on the scent for wickedness is a glory which does good to the heart of any boy. The teacher should look for good, and show that he expects it, and he will rarely find himself disappointed.

11. Threats.—Teachers should never threaten, but if threats are made teachers ought to see them executed. Threats as to what we must do and what we must not do always tend to irritate us. They have much the same effect on children. Many a threat is regarded by the child as simply a challenge, and often children are tempted to wrong-doing by the mere threat which has suggested the evil.

12. Unwise Regulations.—Great care should be exercised in the adoption of regulations, that none be included which are likely to cause pupils to chafe and fret under their restrictions. All regulations that are likely to insinuate that pupils cannot be trusted, or that interfere with their personal freedom where such interference is not necessary for the welfare of the school, should be ex-

cluded. These are not only unnecessary, but also unwise, because they seem unreasonable to the child, and cause him to chafe under their requirements and question their utility and justice. Many a rebellion against authority might be obviated by discarding all such regulations as are not needed for the wise government of the school.

5. Means of Avoiding Disorder.

Disorder may to a great extent be avoided by wisely removing the causes which lead to it, but the teacher does not always have the necessary power to do this. He can do little in the matter of improving either the school-house or the seatings, and he finds his power limited also in other directions. He may, however, by earnest effort do much to turn the minds of his pupils from wrong-doing and disorder and arouse in them a spirit favorable to good discipline. Among the important means of preventing disorder are the following:

1. **The School should be Made Pleasant and Attractive.** —This is one of the first duties of the teacher. Efforts to make the school attractive will prove effective not only in drawing pupils to the school, but also in breaking up irregular attendance and truancy, and in preserving good order while pupils are in school. It is rarely the case that pupils become truants unless they find the fields and the streets more inviting than the school-room. Pleasant employment should be given to every child while at school, and the teacher's manner and instruction should both be so interesting as to attract and hold the attention of the children.

2. **The School-room should be Ornamented.**—This is one of the readiest and most effective means of making the

school pleasant.   Engravings, tasteful pictures, charts, and other ornaments should be hung on the walls. Wherever it is possible pots of growing plants should be placed at the windows, and where this is not possible groups of autumn leaves, dried ornamental grasses, or dried ferns, tastefully arranged, should be made to add to the beauty of the room.   The cabinets of leaves, grasses, minerals, grains, etc. heretofore mentioned may be made to serve the same purpose.   Sets of ornamental mottoes may be made to do double duty in beautifying the room and at the same time instilling valuable moral sentiments.

3. **Pupils should be Encouraged.**—No one can estimate the full effect of kindness and encouragement.   The teacher, above all others, should be cautious to encourage at all times.   The weak are thus strengthened, and the strong made stronger.   Many a failure to do good work is the result of faultfinding where kindness was needed.   Discouraged pupils find a short route to disorder.   The teacher who speaks kind and encouraging words to his pupils rarely finds government a difficult task.

4. **The Teacher should Cultivate a Pleasant and Cheerful Disposition.**—It is the teacher's duty to be cheerful in order that the influence over his pupils may be right.   The sour, sullen, morose dyspeptic is out of place in the school-room. It is the teacher's privilege, as well as his duty, to mingle with his pupils and associate with them.   His disposition should be such, then, as will not tend to lead his pupils to look on the dark side of life, but such rather as will brighten their lives and cheer them on in their work. The cheerful, energetic teacher with a kind word for

every one is a force whose power cannot well be over-estimated.

5. Eternal Vigilance should be Preserved.—Teachers must be wide awake, not only to detect culprits after offenses have been committed, but also to prevent offenses by anticipating mischief. The teacher, as has before been said, should not be a spy, but he should be alive to all that is going on in the school-room, and the mere fact that he is wide awake and watchful to detect mischief before it results in an offense will have a powerful influence in preventing any violation of the school regulations.

6. Pupils should be Kept Busy.—Idlers are the ones who find most opportunities to be disorderly. Busy children rarely have time to devote to mischief. The secret of success in managing small children, as well as larger ones, lies in giving them plenty to do. The criminals who fill our jails as convicts are not the busy, industrious mechanics and laboring-men of a community, however poor these may be, but they are the loungers and idlers who have ample time to plan and mature their mischievous plots and carry them into execution.

7. The Public Opinion of the School must be Made Unfavorable to Disorder.—Public opinion is always powerful in controlling the action of individuals, even where conscience does not make known its disapproval. Every child has more or less regard for the public sentiment of the school. This public sentiment should therefore be trained to indorse the right and condemn the wrong. If such a sentiment can be aroused among the pupils of a school, it will act as a powerful preventive of disorder.

8. The Teacher should Show his Pupils that he has Con

fidence in them.—Confidence begets confidence. We have faith in those who have faith in us. The teacher should never for a moment show that he suspects his pupils of any inclination to do wrong. He will rarely find his confidence misplaced; and even should such be the case, it will be time then to let the children know that he has lost faith in them. It is a rare thing indeed that a child betrays the trust confided to him. Indeed, it is sometimes wise to entrust children with the care of property or assign them special work to do, simply to make them feel that you have faith in them. It will give them a higher opinion of themselves.

9. The Teacher should be Courteous and Polite.—Politeness in the teacher will find its counterpart in the pupil. The teacher who meets his pupils on the street as well as in the school-room with a pleasant smile or a courteous bow will soon find himself surrounded by courteous and polite pupils, who will rarely attempt to give him trouble in school or elsewhere. Besides, this method of treatment will have much to do with making ladies and gentlemen of the children who otherwise would grow up rude and uncivil.

10. The Teacher should Consent Cordially when Favors are Granted.—Few of us care to be accommodated by favors which are bestowed upon us grudgingly. We prefer that those who favor us or comply with our requests should do so cordially. Children do not differ from us in this respect. They dislike to ask the consent of one who accompanies the consent with a growl of reluctance. Indeed, such consent is but little preferable to refusal.

11. The Teacher should Permit the Pupils to do Favors.

—Some of the worst cases of seeming incorrigibility may be reached and cured by permitting the child, or even requesting him, to do favors for you. The fact that you place confidence in him gives him a more exalted opinion not only of himslf, but also of you, and he forthwith determines to be worthy of your good opinion. When the school-room is to be ornamented or errands are to be run, do not always give the work to the good pupils; the others will be quite as anxious to accommodate you. One of the best plans to win the good opinion of the bad boys is to permit them to favor you whenever possible.

12. The Teacher should not Worry.—Worry wears faster than work. A reasonable quantity of work hurts no one, but all worry is more or less unreasonable and hurtful. The worry and fretfulness of the teacher cause the pupils to worry and become fretful. This lays the foundation for disorder, and proper control and discipline of the school are for the time lost. No one has yet succeeded in doing everything he desired. The teacher must of necessity leave much undone. His pupils will now and then fail, and all he can do is to do his best. Overwork brings on worry and excitement, which always prove harmful.

13. Co-education.—The co-education of the sexes is conducive to good order. Boys become less rude and girls less frivolous when in the society of each other. This is particularly true where the two sexes study and recite in the same room under the guidance of a judicious teacher. The presence of each sex has a beneficial effect on the other, not only in preserving good order, but also in giving the members of each more confidence in themselves and greater breadth of thought and culture.

6. Rules and Regulations.

System in school management is a necessity, and a few general regulations may be demanded to preserve system and make the school machinery work smoothly and without friction. The following principles are important:

1. Few Rules should be Made.—All rules with penalties attached are to be avoided as much as possible. They are dangerous, and often suggest an offense to the pupil which otherwise would probably never have been thought of. The more rules the more difficult is the work of governing, for under the rule system every infringement must necessarily be noticed and the proper punishment be inflicted.

2. The Teacher should Seldom Refer to the Rules.—It is sufficient to have the rules known in order that the teacher may have something to resort to in justification of administering punishment at times; but the rule governing the case should not be mentioned except when it is broken. To refer constantly to the school rules is simply to set your pupils to thinking about them and to place temptation before them.

3. Rules should be Reasonable.—School rules should be such as commend themselves to the sound judgment of all. The influence of public sentiment is strong, and if the teacher's rules be such as to win the favorable consideration of both pupils and patrons, he need have little fear that there will be any difficulty in enforcing them. On the other hand, unwise or unnecessary rules tend to chafe and fret the pupils and produce discord and disorder rather than prevent them.

4. Rules should be General in their Character.—School

rules must be general in their application. Special cases can usually be met by special treatment, but in general the rules should be made to apply to all. There may, of course, be individual cases in which the rule should be subject to exceptions, as where the enforcement would be productive of great harm to a nervous or a deformed child. Rules should be general also in their specifications, not pointing out individual offenses and attaching specific penalties except where specially demanded.

5. **Rules should Aim at Securing the Greatest Good.**— They are not to be made for the convenience and comfort of the teacher, but to protect the rights of the pupils and preserve the order and harmony of the school as a whole. Their aim should be to secure the greatest good to the greatest number. Such rules will commend themselves and secure compliance to their requirements, because they are reasonable and wise.

6. **Special Rules should be Adopted only when they become Necessary.**—The teacher who draws up his rules and regulations in advance will find quite as much trouble in attempting to enforce them as he experiences in controlling and directing the school. Indeed, the fewer rules one attempts to enforce the more successful will be his discipline. Pupils soon learn to recognize the fact that the teacher is willing to trust them and has confidence in them, but when they find themselves hedged in on every side by specific rules the natural questions which arise are not, Is this right? Will the teacher approve of it? but rather, Is this prohibited? Is there any rule forbidding it? The teacher is entirely safe in going into school without a single rule, and informing his pupils that he has faith in them that they will try to do what they believe to be

right. Each needed rule may then be made when the necessity for it arises.

7. **Rules should be Such as can be Enforced.**—Such rules as are merely ornamental, and such as are placed in the list merely to frighten pupils, are not only unwise, but also absurd. Among rules of this character may be mentioned all such as affix corporal punishment as a penalty where ability to enforce the rule or administer the punishment depends altogether on the physical development and courage of the teacher. To permit rules to remain on the list without attempting to enforce them or punish when the rules are disobeyed is worse than to have no rules at all.

8. **Rules should not be Inflexible.**—No rules are so mischievous and absurd as those which measure out certain punishments for particular offenses, without taking into consideration the motive or the circumstances which may have led to breaking the rule. Thus, a rule which prohibits all whispering, without inquiring into the motive which caused the violation of the rule, is both unwise and unjust. It recognizes no distinction between innocent infringement of a rule and willful disobedience. The teacher who insists upon inflexible rules, or rather invariable punishments for the violation of rules, will frequently find himself placed in the unpleasant dilemma of being compelled to administer punishment when he knows himself to be doing wrong, or permit a violation of his rules to go unpunished.

9. **The Pupils should be Permitted to Assist in Adopting the Rules.**—It is a good plan when a rule becomes necessary to give the pupils a voice in its adoption. They will rarely abuse their privileges, and when once the rule is

adopted they recognize it as a law of their own making. Their obedience to such rules also becomes more cheerful. The teacher should of course explain to them the necessity for the rule, and lead them to vote for its adoption as a matter of choice. Should there be a few pupils who seem inclined to vote against it, a call of the roll and a vote by *yes* or *no* as each name is called will usually bring them to the side of the majority.

10. **The Teacher should not be Severe in Punishing a Violation of the Rules.**—He should always inquire narrowly into the motive. The child's physical and mental organization should be well considered. The teacher should assure himself that the offense is not the result of some taunt or some physical infirmity; also, that it was willful, and not the result of accident or thoughtlessness. Teacher, see to it that you are cool. Look to all these points; be reasonable and just, and in a majority of cases you will find no necessity for the infliction of punishment.

Suggestions.—1. In making or enforcing rules look back to your own childhood; recall your own experiences, your notions, your impulses. Put yourself in the place of the child to be governed, then act.

2. Regard all pupils as trustworthy until you find them otherwise. Children rarely forgive a teacher who suspects them of wrong when they are innocent.

. 3. Encourage them to be truthful by remitting penalties as far as possible when they make a full and free confession.

4. Common sense and the ability to judge the guilt or innocence of a pupil is a requisite in successful government.

5. Allow pupils the largest liberty consistent with their welfare and the welfare of the school, and when restrictions are placed on them explain the necessity for such restriction.

6. Do not attempt to compel pupils to inform on one another under threats of punishment. Rather let your own tact govern you in the detection of an offense.

7. Explain to your pupils the necessity of proper deportment and prompt obedience.

8. Do your own governing as far as possible; it weakens your authority to call upon the Superintendent or the members of the School Board for assistance.

9. Give no unnecessary commands.

10. Make only such rules as you are willing to enforce.

7. School Punishments.

Both divine and civil government recognize the necessity of punishment as a penalty for wrong-doing. Without the power to punish there can be no government, but the necessity for enforcing punishment should be avoided as far as possible by good school management.

The Objects of School Punishment.

These seem to be of a threefold character, as follows:

1. Reformation of the Offender.
2. Warning to Others.
3. Maintaining the Supremacy of the Law.

Punishments which have other than these ends in view are manifestly improper. No teacher has the right to punish for the mere purpose of gratifying his own temper. The punishment of an offender will deter others from committing a similar offense, while at the same time law and order will be maintained in the school. All laws governing the school must be for the greatest good, and each pupil must be made to feel that the law is supreme and that each owes obedience.

Principles Governing Punishment.

1. **Punishments must be Certain.**—It is the certainty of punishment that prevents offenses. The certainty of even light punishments is more effective than the severity of those applied irregularly. This, too, is the law of Nature. Offenses against our physical system are always attended with bodily pain and discomfort, while those against our moral nature are followed by remorse of conscience.

2. **Punishments should Correspond to the Magnitude of the Offense.**—Here, again, both the moral and the physical laws set the example, and the teacher or the parent who administers punishment will find either to be a safe guide. Slight offenses demand slight punishments, while the graver offenses demand greater severity. It is better, however, in all cases to try the lighter penalties first, and at all times avoid, if possible, great severity. With most children the thought of punishment is often more effective than the punishment itself.

3. **The Physical Condition of the Child should Modify the Severity of Punishment.**—The teacher who would punish a frail, delicate child with the same punishment that he would administer to one who is rugged and of sound physical constitution is little better than a brute. On this same principle also the delicate, sensitive nature of girls should protect them not only against corporal

punishment, but also against all other forms that are likely to make them feel that they have been degraded.

4. Punishment should be Modified According to the Kind of the Offense.—For all violations of laws governing our physical nature we suffer pain, ill-health, or physical discomfort. Violations of laws governing our moral nature bring upon us a different class of punishments and cause us to suffer in a different manner. Here, again, we have an example teaching us that each class of offenses should have its own kind of punishment. At one period in the history of education corporal punishment of some kind was the cure-all for every sort of offense; at another, the dunce-cap was the favorite implement of punishment; at another, detention after school; at another, standing in the corner; and so on. The teacher made no discrimination as to the kind of offense committed, but punished all alike, with but little variation in the degree of punishment and none in the kind.

5. Punishments are Related to Offenses as Effects to Causes.—Here, again, natural laws give us the example. Not only are violations of hygienic laws followed invariably by physical discomfort or ill-health, but the infringement of each law brings its own kind of punishment as the effect of violating that particular law. Undue exposure causes cold, catarrh, pneumonia, and similar diseases. Excessive eating causes indigestion and dyspepsia. Undue nervous excitement or mental application results in nervous prostration and possible insanity. Thus, too, each school offense has its proper penalty, and the child should be made to feel that the penalty is visited upon him as the natural result of his own misconduct, and not as the arbitrary exercise of power vested in the teacher as the

head of the school. The justice of punishments inflicted as the natural effect of the infringement of some school
regulation will be recognized by every pupil, who, if the
punishments are made certain, as they are in Nature,
cannot but feel that when an offense is committed its
appropriate penalty or punishment must follow as the
result of a violation of law.

The Degree of Punishment.

The degree or severity of punishment should not be
arbitrary or governed by the teacher's temper. Every
kind of offense should not only have its proper kind
of punishment, but every grade of the offense should
also have its proper degree of penalty to be inflicted.
The teacher should be governed by the following principles in determining the degree of punishment:

1. **The Degree of Punishment Depends upon the Nature
of the Offense.**—Slight offenses, or those of a nature not
likely to interfere with the welfare of the school or the
teacher, need but slight punishment, while those of a
more serious character and likely to lead to greater violations of the school discipline should be met promptly
with punishment of greater severity.

2. **The Degree of Punishment Depends upon the Motive
of the Offender.**—Many seeming offenses are not meant by
the pupils as offenses at all, and therefore need simply a
caution and no punishment whatever. In a school of
fifty children the teacher must expect considerable life
and no little noise, but he must not think that every act
of thoughtlessness on the part of the children is meant to
interfere with either his discipline or his comfort. Such
offenses are without motive, and in any well-regulated

school they must be expected as surely as we should expect lambs to frisk or birds to sing. The teacher who would punish them with severity would prove himself utterly unfit to have charge of children, and utterly incompetent to fill the post of teacher.

On the other hand, the offense may be committed with the purpose of annoying the teacher, breaking up the good order of the school, injuring other pupils, or some equally malicious purpose. In every such case punishment is necessary, and the severity must be determined not only by the motive, but also by the magnitude and importance of the offense.

3. The Degree of Punishment Depends upon the Frequency of Repetition.—The teacher is sometimes unable to determine the motive which actuates a child in committing an offense for the first time, but when the offense is frequently repeated the question is not so difficult to solve. The first offense, therefore, unless the motive is clearly understood, should not be punished so severely as the same offense when subsequently repeated. The more frequent the repetition also the more severe in general should be the penalty.

4. The Degree of Punishment Depends on the Difficulty of Detection.—The punishment in every case ought to be governed to some extent by the difficulty which the teacher experiences in detecting the offender. Conspiracies in school are always more difficult to detect than open violations of law. They are also more dangerous to school discipline, and the punishment visited upon those who not only commit the offense, but also seek to hide it and their connection with it, should necessarily be more severe than if no effort were made to screen themselves and baffle the teacher in his efforts at detection.

5. The Degree of Punishment Depends on the Age and the Sex of the Offender.—A moderate degree of punishment to a hardy, well-developed youth might prove a great cruelty if inflicted upon a small child or a tender girl. In general, it will be found that mild corporal punishment is much more effective with small children than with older pupils; to the latter an appeal to their sense of honor, a reproof, deprivation of privileges, or placing them where they cannot communicate with their associates, is the most effective punishment. I doubt if girls, particularly those beyond the age of twelve, ever should be subjected to corporal punishment. They may be corrected in other ways much less dangerous, and the wise teacher will refrain from administering to them any bodily punishment, the result of which may be lifelong injury.

6. The Degree of Punishment Depends on the Temperament of the Offender.—The temperaments of children differ as widely as their physical organization, and no teacher can reach all by the same method of procedure. The choleric and the sanguine cannot be governed in the same manner as we would govern the lethargic and the phlegmatic. A nervous, sensitive child requires different discipline from that which we would apply to one of a dull, plodding, lethargic disposition. The degree of the punishment, as well as the kind, must vary according to the varying temperaments. To one whose sense of honor is keen, and who is characterized by great nervous energy, a word of reproof is of more consequence than a sound administering of corporal

punishment to one of an opposite temperament. It is the dull, plodding work-horse that needs the spur as an incentive, and not the lithe-limbed, keen-eyed, fleet-footed Arabian courser.

Kinds of Punishment.

Punishments may properly be divided into two classes: first, *judicious punishments*, which from their nature are well adapted to secure the objects of punishment as heretofore stated; and second, *injudicious punishments*, or such as tend to defeat one or more of the true ends of punishment.

1. **Judicious Punishments.**—Of judicious punishments the following seem to be the most important:

1. **Reproof.**—This is of a threefold nature—*general reproof*, *private reproof*, and *public reproof*. It may vary greatly in degree, but it should never degenerate into scolding. When properly administered, it will usually be found effective in showing to the child his faults, and at the same time influence him to correct them.

General Reproof is the first to be tried. It is also the mildest in its nature, and in the hands of a good disciplinarian it is usually effective. It consists simply in the nature of a general statement that a certain offense has been committed, without the mention of any one's name, but accompanied with the request kindly made and the hope earnestly expressed that the offense will not be repeated. It is wise often to go so far even as to suggest the opinion that the offense was not committed willfully, but was probably the result of thoughtlessness, or possibly of accident. Pupils thus kindly dealt with rarely fail to comply with the teacher's wishes, and the plan is found to operate quite as satisfactorily with young men and women in higher-grade schools as with children.

Private Reproof consists in a private interview with the offender, and it may vary very greatly in its character. It may consist in showing to the pupil the nature and gravity of the offense he has committed, with a demand that he shall do better in the future, with an earnest statement also as to what the future consequences may be if the offense is repeated; or it may consist of a kindly talk in which the teacher convinces the pupil of his friendship, takes him by the hand, offers to help him avoid future trouble, asks him in behalf of himself, his parents, and the school to do better, encourages rather than chides, points out the better way, and lends a guiding hand to direct. What nature will not be subdued by such treatment? What boy's heart, however flinty, may not be softened by kind, gentle, and affectionate advice? Private reproof kindly administered cannot fail to win the esteem of the child.

Public Reproof should be administered only when the offense committed is of the gravest possible nature. When an offense is committed in such a way as to defy the authority of the teacher public reproof is permissible. Public opinion of the school is powerful as a discipline, and cases may occur where the position of the teacher can be understood and appreciated only by a public statement, in order that misrepresentations made by the offender may be corrected. In such cases public reproof becomes necessary; also, where there exists a false sympathy with one who has openly defied the school discipline.

In general, public reproof of a single individual is a

dangerous punishment, and the teacher ought to avoid it
The pupil should be trained to self-respect, and great care
should be taken that the desire for the good opinion of
his associates be kept alive and active. Public reproof
should be resorted to only after general reproof and private reproof have failed.

2. **Reparation of Damages.**—It seems but just that
when injury is done to property, whether public or
private, the person who does the injury should pay for
the damage done; and this same rule should hold in
schools as elsewhere.

3. **Performance of Neglected Duties.**—When duties are
neglected by pupils it is right and proper that they
should be performed during such time as may be appropriated to play or recreation. An unstudied lesson
should be studied, because of its connection with what
precedes or follows, and such study may justly be required of the pupil as a punishment for his neglect; and
thus also of other neglected work.

4. **Deprivation of Privileges.**—It is always proper
when privileges are abused that we should be deprived
of those privileges. In school life these privileges are
many, and this method of punishment becomes therefore of considerable importance. Restraint is as necessary in school government as in the state, and the teacher
should have power to apply it whenever necessary for
the general good of the school. Of the many privileges
which the pupil may forfeit by improper conduct, the
following may be named as among the most important:

a. **Recess.**—Those who constantly annoy their play-mates or interfere with the comforts of others during play-time, as well as those who are apt to be profane or vulgar in their use of language on the play-ground, might with propriety be detained at recess, and be permitted to have their recess after the other pupils have returned to study.

b. **Forfeiture of Seat.**—This is a proper punishment for those who annoy their neighbors by talking, shaking the desk, or causing interruptions and annoyance by other means.

c. **Dismissal from Recitation.**—The pupil ought to feel it a privilege to recite with his classmates. Certain conduct is improper in the class-room because detrimental to the interests of the class as a whole and to the individual members. Among the kinds of improper conduct during recitation may be named the following: *Whispering, prompting others, copying from others, annoying classmates, disturbing the class or the teacher by noise, rude and impertinent answers, boisterous behavior, and inattention;* for all or any of which the teacher may properly dismiss a pupil from recitation, and demand a special recitation when he is not engaged in other work.

Should the class be disturbed by ill-behaved pupils, it is best for the teacher to act promptly, stopping all work for the time until pupils become quiet and orderly; and if the disorderly ones do not become quiet at once, they may be dismissed for the time. For continued misconduct of this kind the pupil may properly be placed in a lower class, and thus lose his class-standing, which is a loss of privilege in itself.

d. **Detention after School.**—In the hands of a judicious

14

teacher this punishment may be used, but it is, to say the least, a dangerous form of punishment. ⸲ For pupils who are guilty of misconduct on their way home from school, or who are inclined to quarrel with their schoolmates, detention for ten or fifteen minutes, so as to deprive them of the companionship of their associates, seems entirely appropriate.   Pupils should not, however, be detained after school hours as a general thing for mischief committed during school hours or for failure of lessons.   There are other punishments more appropriate to these offenses.   When pupils are detained after school the teacher should never leave the school-room until all the pupils have first been dismissed and sent to their homes.

Two serious objections may be urged against detention after school.   The first is that the school hours are already too long for the health and comfort of the children; and the second, that the detention of pupils necessarily involves also the detention of the teacher.

e. **Withdrawal of Favors.**—The approval of the teacher is always a strong incentive to good conduct.   No more severe punishment can be inflicted on the pupil than the withdrawal of this approval.   We are all glad to be praised, and when this praise is withdrawn and censure made to take its place, we feel the punishment keenly.   This is a punishment to be inflicted only when the pupil shows himself to be deceitful and unworthy of confidence.

5. **Private Apology.**—It is always proper to apologize for a wrong done.   Every properly-disposed pupil will recognize the justice of a punishment of this kind.   If

he has done an injury to a fellow-pupil, either accidentally or purposely, it would be proper for him to apologize. If he does this freely, in many cases no further punishment should be administered, but where the injury to another has resulted in loss to him it would be proper also to make reparation for damage done. Private apology to the teacher is also an effective punishment in many cases where the offense strictly merits a much more severe form of punishment, but where greater good can be accomplished by substituting the milder for the more severe.

6. Public Apology.—This is a punishment which is admissible in extreme cases. Most pupils would prefer to leave school rather than rise to make public acknowledgment of their wrong-doing and apologize for the offense. Where a wrong to a pupil or the school has been done publicly, justice demands that the offender make a public apology; and yet even here a more judicious form of punishment might be administered, and in such a way as to benefit the guilty as well as the innocent. Particularly is this a doubtful punishment to apply in the government of students who have passed from the age of childhood to that of youth.

7. Personal Chastisement.—In placing personal chastisement or bodily punishment under the head of judicious punishments I am aware that I shall meet with some little opposition of sentiment; but with all the arguments offered on both sides my personal experience warrants me in saying that the power to punish by the infliction of bodily pain is usually a great check on misconduct, even though that power be but rarely exercised.

a. **Definition.**—*Corporal punishment* is the inflicting of bodily pain for the purpose of correcting offenses. It may consist of punishment by means of a rod or other instrument, this being the usual means, but it includes all kinds of punishment where the child is made to suffer physical pain or discomfort as a means of reform.

b. **The Right of the Teacher to Punish.**—The law recognizes the teacher as being in place of the parent. Whatever rights the parent has under the circumstances are delegated for the time to the teacher. Neither dare punish with undue severity without making himself amenable to the law. Where no statute exists the law of custom gives to the teacher the right and power to punish within certain limits. By some local School Boards, and indeed by some States, this power is denied to the teacher.

c. **The Law of Prohibition.**—The law which prohibits the teacher from using corporal punishment is of doubtful expediency. It is true, many teachers punish unwisely and with too great frequency, but there seems to be no good reason why the hands of a faithful teacher should be tied because incompetents abuse the power entrusted to them. It were better to dismiss persons who cannot govern without corporal punishment, and let this be held as the last reserve force to be used by the competent teacher, the pupils understanding that the teacher has the power to inflict this kind of punishment in extreme cases.

d. **The Better Plan.**—A better plan than that of prohibiting corporal punishment by law would be to have teachers report at the close of each month to the School Board or to the Superintendent the number of cases in which corporal punishment has been inflicted during the month, together with the offense for which the pupil was punished. Many a teacher would be ashamed of his record, and the number reported would grow rapidly less. This would cause a practical abolition of corporal punishment, and yet the power and its moral effect would remain as an incentive to good behavior.

e. Corporal Punishment of Doubtful Expediency.—This kind of punishment is the weapon of the weak teacher. One whose experience has taught him to govern by higher and better motives rarely, if ever, finds it necessary to use corporal punishment. It is always likely to provoke the hostility of parents and involve the teacher in difficulties. Indeed, there is great danger of losing the esteem and good-will of both pupils and parents. There is probably no method of punishment liable to greater abuse, or one where greater cruelty or revenge may be visited upon a pupil under the disguise of kindness and necessity. It is a matter of some difficulty to convince children that you whip them because you love them and because it is necessary, and it is quite as difficult sometimes to convince yourself of the fact.

f. Principles Governing the Use of Corporal Punishment. —Corporal punishment should be used only in extreme cases, and then only in accordance with the following principles:

1. It should be Moderate.—The law wisely protects the child from all manner of cruel punishment. If punishment is administered as a corrective, there is no necessity for extreme severity. The moral effect will be quite as good though the pain be not so great.

2. It should be Administered in Private.—Private punishment is more effective than public, but corporal

punishment should be administered in the presence of a witness or two, though it be administered privately, in order that the child may not misrepresent both the teacher's manner and the severity of the punishment, as he might if no witnesses were present.

3. **It should be Deliberate.**—The teacher should never punish when angry. A day's reflection on the matter may give him an entirely different view of the case, and all necessity for punishment may possibly be avoided, or the pupil may repent of his wrong and be willing to submit to any other proper punishment. When angry the teacher may punish too severely, and thus entirely destroy the moral effect of the punishment.

4. **The Instrument of Punishment should be Appropriate.** —The choice is usually a switch or a rod. Either of these is liable, under the most favorable circumstances, to leave marks and furnish the basis for prosecutions and lawsuits. A better implement would be one which, while it causes quite as much pain, does not leave ridges or marks on the skin. A flat ferule or a piece of lath answers the purpose admirably.

5. **Punishment should be Administered on the Muscular Parts of the Body.**—This needs little argument. All other parts of the body are liable to injury. Even the shoulders are not a proper portion of the body to receive punishment, because of the fact that punishment applied here may cause serious nervous diseases.

6. **Punishment should Never be Inflicted on the Head or the Hands.**—All punishment inflicted on the head or the ears is cruel. Pulling the ears, striking the head with a book, and similar punishments, are extremely dangerous. Punishing on the hands is but little better. The hand,

as the organ of touch, is too sensitive to admit of punishment without danger of lifelong injury.

Cautions on Corporal Punishment.

Observe the following cautions in administering corporal punishment:

1. *Be Certain of the Pupil's Guilt before Punishing.*—Never punish until you have looked on all sides of the case and convinced yourself beyond a doubt that the offender is guilty. If there be any doubt, give the pupil the benefit of that doubt.

2. *Postpone Punishment until You can Administer it Coolly and Deliberately.*—If you do not change your determination entirely, your punishment will be at least much more lenient and much more reasonable.

3. *Consult with the Child's Parents if the Punishment is to be Severe.*—This may save you much trouble and future embarrassment. The parent may be willing to inflict the punishment himself, and thus relieve you of much responsibility. Of course cases demanding immediate attention must be an exception.

4. *Appeal to the Sense of Honor First.*—If there seems a necessity for corporal punishment, it is always safe to appeal to the child's sense of honor before deciding to administer punishment. He may be thoroughly repentant, and anxious to do better and make amends for his offense, in which case the punishment becomes unnecessary.

5. *Inflict Corporal Punishment Publicly only when the Offense is a Willful Defiance of Authority.*—In such case the punishment may be administered without delay and in the presence of the school. If the pupils are well-disposed they will indorse your action.

6. *After the Punishment Treat the Pupil Kindly.*— Nothing will do more to convince him of his wrong action speedily than showing him you punished not from choice, but from necessity; and this you can best show by restoring the offender to your favor immediately after the punishment.

8. Suspension.—Among the judicious punishments is a temporary suspension from school privileges. This is a punishment which is liable to do great injury to the child, and it should be used among the very last. A blot seems to go with the suspension which often mars the record of one's life.

The chief *causes which would justify suspension* are the following, but it is not argued that suspension should take place in every case here cited:

1. Insubordination.—Pupils may be so unwilling to to submit to the regulations of a school that they interfere with its welfare. They may destroy, or seek to destroy, its good name. They may be inclined to create rebellion and strife, and enter into a conspiracy to break down the teacher's authority. In such cases the teacher has the undoubted right to suspend the offenders.

2. Truancy.—While a confirmed habit of irregular attendance justifies the teacher in suspending the offender on the ground of retarding the progress of the school, great care should be exercised in applying the penalty. The danger is that of suspending on too slight provocation. Every other means should be used to secure regular attendance and break up truancy before resorting to suspension. Indeed, this is simply an acknowledgment on the part of the teacher that he cannot secure regular

attendance, and therefore prefers not to receive the irregular pupils.

3. Gross Misconduct.—Pupils of immoral character are out of place in the ordinary school. Those possessed of habits which in a grown person would send him to prison ought to be consigned to reform schools or houses of correction. We cannot be too careful as to the moral character of the associates of our children. The seeds of moral poison are often sown in the school-room and on the play-ground without detection under the very eye of the teacher.

4. Habitual Idleness.—Of this fault also it may be said that while a teacher would be justifiable in suspending a confirmed idler, it is of doubtful policy to use the power so long as there is a possible means left of reclaiming the child and interesting him in the school work.

The Power to Suspend.—This power belongs to the teacher. He is the governor and ruler of the school, and the power is rightly placed in his hands. Were it otherwise, a faithful teacher might constantly be annoyed by the utter worthlessness of some pupils, and yet be powerless to conduct his school properly and rid it of the disturbing elements, because of the negligence or refusal to act on the part of those in whom the right of suspension might be vested. The laws of some States give to the teacher the right to suspend for an indefinite time until the pupil is reinstated by the Board of Directors.

When the teacher finds it necessary to suspend a pupil, it is better that it be done quietly and without the knowledge of the school. So far as the school is concerned, it will have quite as beneficial an effect as if done publicly;

and as regards the student suspended, a chance is given him to redeem himself in the future. The suspension can of course be announced publicly, but the effect is to make a target of the unfortunate pupil, and the stigma clings to him for a lifetime. Public defiance of authority and vicious persistence, and but little else than these, ought to be considered good ground for public suspension.

Length of the Sentence.—This must be governed largely by the cause which leads to suspension. The sentence should not be so brief as to make it of no effect, nor should it be so extended as to bring the school or the teacher into contempt and subject the latter to the charge of suspending for spite. Reformation is what is desired, and as soon as the pupil is willing to make proper acknowledgments his sentence should be removed and he be permitted to resume his place in school. Teachers in public schools have not always the power to fix the length of sentence; this, then, should be done by the School Board, but always in such a way as to sustain the teacher when he is right.

When a pupil is readmitted the teacher should never show, either by act or word, that the past in his conduct is remembered. We wander too far sometimes from the true Christian standard in condemning the one who has sinned. We should rather put out a helping hand to him who is trying to redeem his reputation and regain his place in the esteem of the teacher and the school.

9. **Expulsion.**—Suspension, as has been explained, is a temporary sentence. Expulsion severs the pupil's connection with the school permanently, unless the

school authorities should see fit to reinstate him by withdrawing the sentence. Expulsion can hardly be said to be a reformatory punishment, for the reason that the sentence shuts off the pupil permanently from all school privileges. It has for its object the good of the school alone, as capital punishment has the good of the state.

The *offenses* which may be taken as a just cause for expulsion are of the gravest possible nature. The following are the chief:

1. **Gross Immorality.**—A student whose moral character is so debased as likely to work evil to the remainder of the school, or whose conduct is if such a character as to be a pernicious example, ought not to be permitted to remain in school. Particularly is this true if he be found incorrigible.

2. **A Constant Disregard for the School Regulations.**— All students are likely now and then to infringe school regulations thoughtlessly. Occasionally there are students who habitually disobey from a spirit of rebellion. These should be met with firmness and be expelled at once. No act is more justifiable than that of expulsion for a determined opposition to the school's interests, whether as the result of individual malice or of conspiracy and rebellion.

3. **Dangerous Conduct.**—Under the head of "dangerous conduct" may be included such malicious mischief as impels a pupil to destroy the school furniture and do injury to the school-house and the school property; also the habit of speaking evil of the school. Such conduct on the part of a pupil as is likely to destroy the harmony of the school, break down its regulations, interfere with

the rights of other students to a great extent, is justifiable cause for expulsion.   All such conduct is dangerous
to the school interests, and expulsion may be applied as
the punishment, though sentence should be passed only
after all means of reform have on trial proved a failure.

Who may Expel.—This power is reserved to the School
Boards in public schools.   In normal schools, and sometimes, though rarely, in graded schools, the power is
vested in the principal and the faculty.   Teachers in
ungraded schools may, under the laws of most States,
suspend, but not expel.

Cautions.—1. Expulsion may do the student a lifelong
injury.   The blot is difficult to efface.   Never expel,
therefore, until all means of reforming the offender have
first been tried and found inefficient.

2. Do not publish to the world the fact that you have
expelled a student.   It is ungenerous to put an obstacle
of this kind in the way of one who may afterward try
to redeem himself.

3. When necessary to dismiss a student from school,
do it quietly and without the knowledge of his schoolmates, unless the case is of such a character as to demand
exposure.

4. Notify other schools of the expulsion only when
you think it necessary for the purpose of protecting
them against a student of vicious habits or dangerous
character.

5. Be sure before you expel that your student is guilty
and dangerous to the welfare of the school.

10. Deportment Marks.—As to whether these constitute
a judicious punishment or otherwise is a debatable ques-

tion. Each side of this question is advocated by prominent teachers. The objections against deportment marks, however, seem to be urged almost wholly against injudicious and unjust marking. The system has its merits, and these ought not to be overlooked and set aside because extremists abuse the system by marking down for every conceivable offense, imaginary or real, intentional or innocent.

The *basis* of this marking should be a percentage, making 100 as the standard of *perfect* conduct; between 90 and 100, *excellent;* between 80 and 90, *good;* between 70 and 80, *medium;* and below 70, *unsatisfactory.* In reporting to the parent it is held by many teachers that only the words *perfect, excellent, good, medium,* etc. should be reported, so that the special percentages may not be compared and thus create dissatisfaction among the children or the families of the neighborhood.

Deportment marks are a strong incentive to good conduct. Many pupils obey the school regulations because they desire to present a good report to their parents. Let it be granted that the incentive is not one of those to be highly commended, it still has the force of an incentive, as it wins for them the approbation of parents and friends when the record is favorable, and the children are induced to make a favorable record by good conduct where higher motives might have no influence.

2. Injudicious Punishments.—The number of injudicious punishments is very great. All of them ought to be avoided under all circumstances. The following may be named as the most prominent:

1. Scolding.—This is never a proper punishment. Indeed, a scolding teacher soon loses the respect of his pupils. The less the teacher scolds and the less he threatens, the greater the number of friends he will have among his students, and the easier will he find the discipline. When threats are made they should be executed without fail. Both scolding and threats soon lose all force except to irritate a class and make it noisy and disrespectful.

2. Ridicule.—The teacher has no right to ridicule either the defects or the mistakes of a child. Such conduct makes a teacher deserving of all the contempt that pupils can heap upon him. It is the teacher's business to encourage, not to discourage—to help to correct mistakes and train the pupils, instead of making sport of them. Sarcastic remarks with reference to a pupil's ability, calling him a dunce, a numskull, an ignoramus, or other equally offensive names, is contemptible conduct in the teacher.

3. Confinement.—Solitary confinement in a cell is among the most severe of prison punishments, and it is applied only to hardened criminals. Shutting a child in a closet, putting him in the coal-cellar, and like punishments, are no less cruel. To a child of vivid fancy or nervous organization serious injury may be wrought by a punishment of this kind. Solitary confinement is not only injudicious as a school punishment, but it is also unwise.

4. Personal Indignities.—Among personal indignities may be mentioned all those annoying punishments which, though not severe in themselves, serve to irritate a child, such as pulling the ears, snapping the head, pull-

ing the hair, compelling the child to wear a dunee-cap, and the like. All of them are improper.

5. **Personal Torture.**—All kinds of torture are improper punishments. Many of the old-fashioned punishments were little less than barbarous. Such punishments·as compelling a child to stand on one foot, hold a book at arm's length, kneel on the sharp edge of a piece of wood, walk barefooted on peas, hold a nail in the floor without bending the knee, etc., ought to belong to the Dark Ages.

6. **Performance of Tasks for Misconduct.**—No pupil should ever be asked to study a lesson for misconduct. There is no connection between the two, and a love for learning is not instilled in this way. The boy who-is required to write two hundred words after school as a punishment for pinching his neighbor or whispering in school does not see the relation of the punishment to the offense, and he must come to regard his teacher in the true light, as being either tyrannical or ignorant of the art of school discipline.

7. **Degradation of the Offender.**—No pupil has ever been reformed bv degrading him. One of the chief ends of punishment ıs reformation, but this end is directly defeated by attempting to visit on the pupil a punishment which will degrade him either in the eyes of his associates or in his own estimation. His self-respect must be cultivated, not destroyed. Teachers who subject pupils to degrading punishments are inhuman in their nature, and they should not be employed in any school.

8. **Worrying a Pupil.**—The teacher has no right to worry his pupils by irritating or vexatious talk. The

kind of grumbling in which some teachers indulge
hardly rises to the dignity of scolding. It is rather
of the nature of faultfinding. If the child makes a
mistake, the teacher is sure to complain. If he is
guilty of some trivial offense, the teacher has an unkind remark to thrust at him. His conduct toward the
pupil has a constant tendency to vex the child, and
make him feel that the teacher glories in his mistakes
and shortcomings.

9. **Vindictive Punishments.**—Here, again, the teacher
forgets the objects of punishment. The aim of punishment is not to gratify one's ill-temper or revenge, and
the teacher must not punish in a spirit of this kind. It
is safe, therefore, to say that he should never punish
when angry, because all angry punishment is more or
less vindictive.

10. **Cruel Punishments.**—All punishments that exceed
the limits of moderation must be avoided. The statutes
of most States make cruelty of punishment a penal
offense for which the teacher may be indicted. But
cruel punishments do harm also by lessening the respect
of both pupils and patrons for the teacher and his
methods of government.

Cautions.—1. Do not make threats of punishment in
advance.

2. Adapt the punishment to the offense.

3. Do not try to make pupils learn by whipping for
unlearned lessons.

4. Never inflict a punishment which is likely to make
a pupil feel that he ought to resent it.

5. Seek to use the minimum of punishment.

6. Be patient with the shortcomings of your pupils.

7. Do your utmost to prevent faults, so as to avoid the necessity of punishment.

8. Punish only for willful misconduct.

9. Do not reprove those who try but fail.

10. Do not expect perfect order in the school-room; children are children.

8. How to Detect Offenders.

The detection of offenders, particularly among older pupils, is not only a delicate task, but sometimes also one of great difficulty. Smaller pupils are usually open and confiding in their nature, and an offense committed by them is not difficult to detect. But among the larger pupils there is a disposition to avoid informing on a fellow-student—sometimes because of a false sense of honor, sometimes because the one who should inform is afraid of making an enemy of the one on whom he informs. This disposition to conceal the faults of others makes the difficulty of detection all the greater.

Several methods of detecting offenders are here given, each of which may be used under varying circumstances. The duty of detection is unpleasant, but the teacher who expects to sustain himself must at least make every effort in his power to ferret out the guilty:

1. By Private Confession.—One method of detection is to make before the whole school a statement of the offense committed, and then invite the person guilty of the offense to meet the teacher at his convenience and confess to the fault, with the prospect of a full pardon. Pupils who have confidence in the teacher, or who may have committed the offense thoughtlessly, may often be induced in this manner to confess. Much will depend on the way in which the teacher receives the pupil who comes to confess, and much also on the manner in which the teacher presents the matter to the school. The pupil who comes to confess a fault has already made reparation. He needs no further punishment, and the teacher should speak with him kindly and grant him a full pardon.

2. By Negative Questions.—A very effective method of detecting an offense is to ask of the whole school their connection with the offense by putting the question in the negative form. To illustrate: Suppose an offense has been committed; the teacher should not ask, "Who did this? Who committed this offense?" but rather say, "Those who know nothing about this offense, or who do not know who committed it, may rise." These should be dismissed to some other part of the room. Those who do not rise confess that they know something about it. The second question or statement should then come as follows: "Those who did not commit this offense or help to commit it may rise." There are few, indeed, who would, if guilty, have the hardihood to rise under such circumstances. Experience has proved this to be one of the most satisfactory, and at the same time certain, methods of detecting the guilty.

3. By Private Interview.—Should both of the preceding methods fail, the teacher may ask a private interview with such students as circumstances seem to point out as the guilty parties. There are always some pupils in the school whose general character and conduct is such as to lead them into mischief. There are others also who are always conscientious in their observance of the school regulations. The private interview need in-

clude the former class only, and in many cases, if the teacher proceed judiciously, asking questions but making no direct charges, he will reach the truth. Few will have the boldness to make false statements and attempt to adhere to them without entangling themselves in their testimony.

4. By Public Questions.—This plan proceeds by calling each pupil in turn to rise, and, while looking the teacher in the eye, answer such questions in the presence of the school as the teacher may see fit to ask. Should the teacher fail to detect the offender by this plan, he will still secure considerable valuable evidence, if his questions be judicious, which will be of much service to him in future efforts to fix the guilt on the proper person. Only the gravest offenses justify this method of detection, and the teacher should use it only when he finds all other methods fail.

5. By Giving Time for Reparation.—This is not a method of detection exactly, but rather a preliminary proceeding by which the unpleasantness of searching for the offender may sometimes be avoided. It consists in making a public statement that a certain offense—as, for instance, the taking of a book—has been committed, and that a certain time will be allowed for its return, but if not returned at the time specified, search will be made and the guilty party receive such punishment as the offense merits.

6. By Seeking Information of Well-disposed Pupils.— Tattling and tale-bearing are justly despised by pupils, but that is a false sense of honor which induces pupils to take the ground that they ought neither to confess to their own guilt nor report the guilt of others. There are certain offenses which when committed must interfere more or less with the welfare of a school, and ultimately destroy its good name. These include all malicious mischief, destruction of school furniture, theft, vandalism of all kinds, conspiracy, rebellion, and other offenses equally grave. No well-disposed student should hesitate for a moment to assist the teacher in detecting the perpetrators of such malicious deeds, and every teacher ought to feel himself entirely safe in calling to his aid the most reliable students of his school for the purpose of exposing the guilty. Pupils should be trained to feel that where the interests of the school are imperiled the honorable course is to save the school and expose and convict those who would be guilty of destroying it.

7. **By Constant Vigilance.**—Under certain circumstances all the preceding methods may fail. There is then nothing left but constant vigilance on the part of the teacher. He need not be suspiciously watchful, but no opportunity for gathering evidence should be permitted to pass. The teacher should keep his own secrets. The explanation he confidentially makes to a trusted student may reach the guilty one's ears in an incredibly short time. Silence and vigilance should be his watchwords. In many cases the guilt will come to the surface gradually, and when every link in the chain of evidence is perfect the exposure is sure to follow.

9. The Self-Reporting System.

This system consists in having pupils at the close of the day each rise as their respective names are called and make a confession of the various faults they have committed during the day. By some teachers the particular faults to be confessed are specified; as, for instance, the number of times the child has talked to his associates or the number of times he has made any unnecessary noise.

The System Unwise.—A serious objection to this system is that the good pupils report faithfully, and are marked accordingly, while the evil-disposed report untruthfully, and receive greater credit than the good.

A second serious objection to this system is that it trains the children to be liars. Feeling that those who report the fewest faults are they who will receive the best marks and reports, irrespective of conduct, it is a short step, for even an honest pupil, from truth to falsehood; and even those who have always been accounted truthful have such temptations placed before them that, with the weakness incident to the moral nature of childhood, they in many cases become untruthful.

Confessing a Fault to the Teacher should be encouraged, but any system of confession which charges guilt to the pupil who confesses, and credits the guilty with good behavior, is to be condemned as faulty in principle and vicious in practice. The schools are indeed few in which weak human nature can stand such a strain on conscience as is placed upon it by the so-called *self-reporting system.*

10. Pardons.

School government, from its very nature, must have connected with it the power to pardon those who are repentant. This power may of course be abused and the teacher become too lenient, while, on the other hand, he may be so anxious to show himself just, and may adhere so rigidly to rules, that his government becomes cruel. Justice should always be tempered with mercy.

Two pupils may commit the same fault in school—the first thoughtlessly and without any bad motive, the second out of pure malice; the thoughtless pupil is sorry for his deed, the second is malicious. Do both deserve the same punishment? It would be an unjust teacher indeed who would not pardon the first and punish the second. The pardoning power must, however, be used under certain conditions. These are—

1. **That the Guilty Party give Evidence of Repentance.** —The pupil who manifests no sorrow for a wrong act has, of course, no claims on the teacher for forgiveness or pardon. Any repentance must be sincere and not feigned in order to escape punishment. A feigned repentance of one, and a consequent pardon, will be the example which others will gladly imitate.

2. **That he Apologizes to Those he has Wronged.**—A pupil who is repentant will not hesitate to apologize to any one he may have wronged in committing an offense. This is one of the evidences of repentance. The teacher must not be too exacting as to the language in which this apology is made. Should the child say of his own accord, *I am sorry*, it may mean more than the profoundest apology of one better skilled in the use of language. Without this apology to those he has wronged no pardon should be granted.

3. **That he Make Reparation of Damages.**—There may be circumstances where it is of course impossible to make any reparation, as where personal injury is done to another. In such case the offender's repentance and his willingness to apologize must be taken as evidence of his willingness to make reparation were such a thing possible. In all cases, however, where reparation is

possible, as where injury has been done to the school property or the property of other pupils, it should be made one of the conditions on which pardon is granted.

11. Punishment of Offenses.

It will be sufficient here to name the chief offenses which pupils may be likely to commit in school, together with the appropriate punishment to be applied to each offense. Many other offenses may be committed, but they will not vary in principle to any extent from those here named, and the details of the punishment are best left to the individual judgment and good sense of the teacher.

1. Offenses against Property.—These may be against school property or against the property of others. They may also be either accidental or malicious. When the injury is accidental the pupil may be required to restore the property or pay for the damage done. His own sense of honor will also lead him to apologize to the owner. If the injury be done out of malice, it is not only necessary that the pupil make proper reparation or payment of damages, but he might also be made to apologize for his offense, not only to the owner of the property, but also to the teacher. Injury to his own property is naturally followed by a punishment in the loss of the property. In addition to this, reproof from the teacher would be proper, and the offense should be reported to the parents of the child which does the wrong.

2. Personal Injury.—This may consist of a personal

injury either to schoolmates, to visitors, or to the pupil himself. A personal injury to a schoolmate may be punished by a reproof if the injury be slight, and if of a more serious nature by the deprivation of privileges. Pupils who quarrel or fight at recess or at other times may with propriety be shut away from their schoolmates during playtime, on the ground that they are likely to interrupt the harmony of the plays and do personal injury. An apology required to be made to the person injured would seem in the case of injury to schoolmates to be an appropriate method of punishment.

Injury to strangers passing by, or to visitors, may be punished in the same manner as personal injury to schoolmates. Injury to one's self brings with it its own punishment, and need have no correction, unless, indeed, the offense be in the nature of disobedience as well as personal injury.

3. Accessory to Injury.—Many offenses are committed by those who are instigated by others more cunning than themselves. The pupil who plots mischief, or who directs or requests another to engage in mischief, is equally guilty with the one who perpetrates the deed. Both, therefore, should receive the same punishment in kind and degree.

4. Temptation to Wrong-doing.—No one is more dangerous to the welfare and harmony of a school than a pupil who by his bad example or by personal influence tempts other pupils to do wrong. Young children usually imitate the elder ones in their vices much more certainly than they do in their virtues. A vicious pupil

may do infinite harm by his example, and he needs punishment, not only because of his offense, but also because by his offense he leads others into vice. It is mainly by example that children learn profanity, vulgarity, lying, and other evil habits equally offensive. A pupil who is inclined to tempt others to do wrong ought to be debarred from associating with them. Should this punishment not prove effective, suspension from school should be the next resort, and in extreme cases it would be proper to expel.

5. **Laziness and Inattention.**—Under this may be included negligence in the preparation of the lesson as well as inattention in class. For the former it would be proper to punish by requiring the pupil to prepare his neglected lesson during playtime. For inattention in class, if willful, dismissal from the class and requiring the inattentive pupil to recite by himself usually effects a cure; but in the milder form, where inattention has become a habit, calling on the pupil frequently to recite when he is least attentive often produces good results and in time corrects the bad habit.

6. **Uncouth Manners.**—This fault is usually the result of associating with uncouth companions. Sometimes it is the example of parents repeated in the child's life and manners. Children that come from uncouth homes are necessarily more or less impolite in behavior. Kindness of teacher and pupils, with good example, will do much to correct the evil. A quiet suggestion from the teacher occasionally made in a friendly way will be appreciated and complied with.

7. **Improper Habits.**—These are manifold. They include spitting on the floor, walking heavily, using tobacco, etc. The milder forms of these habits may often be corrected by a mere suggestion on the part of the teacher as to the impropriety of the habit. Some of these evils, however, cannot be reached in this manner. Among these is the habit of using tobacco in the school-room. Both this and spitting on the floor may be corrected by having the pupil either use a spittoon, to be cleansed by him daily, or by requiring offenders to clean the floor daily. Both of these offensive habits ought to be thoroughly broken up, the teacher being careful to set the example.

The habit of walking heavily over the floor is usually the result of thoughtlessness. It may sometimes be corrected by a mere request or a suggestion. If this fail, it may be corrected by having the pupil go back to the starting-point and walk across the floor several times in succession until he learns to walk quietly. Pupils who pass to and from class noisily will see the propriety of their being sent back to come quietly every time they commit the offense.

8. **Immoral Conduct.**—Possibly there are few schools in which there is not some immorality. Some pupils are guilty of vulgarity, some of profanity, some of intemperance. Each of these vices should be dealt with promptly and firmly as soon as detected, and the punishment should be such as to leave no doubt as to the teacher's disapproval and hatred of these offenses. The first punishment to be applied is the deprivation of privileges. Vulgar and profane pupils should be made to

understand that they are not fit associates for their schoolmates, and consequently must be separated from them.   Personal chastisement of any kind rarely succeeds in correcting immoral conduct.   Where separation and reproof do not effect a cure, it is better to lay the case before the School Board and request the removal of the offending pupils.

9. Rude Behavior.—This includes all attempts at annoying either the school or the teacher, such as shuffling the feet on the floor, unnecessary coughing, pushing other pupils from the seat, answering in loud tones of voice, making unnecessary noise with the chairs or the desks; also, incivility to strangers either in the school-room or on the street.   In all such cases it would be proper to demand an apology of the offender, to be made to the person who has been uncivilly treated.   Noise may be made without the intention of annoying the school.   In such cases a slight reproof or a request that the noise be discontinued will usually be sufficient.   But where the noise is indulged in purposely, the pupil, if in class, should be dismissed and be directed to recite his lessons privately at such time as the teacher may find convenient.

The teacher in class may often secure good order by stopping class-exercises for a few moments until all become quiet.   In such cases he should be entirely dignified and preserve his temper unruffled.   Usually, a class will become quiet at once, when he should immediately proceed with the lesson, without taking up a moment's time to scold or refer to the interruption.   In extreme cases he may call upon the offender in a quiet and dignified way, mentioning the pupil's name and requesting that he keep quiet. If the teacher is sure of the pupil's guilt, he should permit no saucy or impertinent retorts, on penalty of punishment for disrespect. Severe reproof may be administered to those who purposely disturb the order of the school.

10. **Theft.**—Pupils frequently appropriate to their own use the property of others without appreciating the enormity of the offense they have committed. In such cases a mild reproof and a restoration of the property taken are all that is required. When, however, the property of others is taken with a full knowledge of the nature of the wrong, the punishment should be more severe. The property should of course be restored, or, if that be not possible, then its value instead. It would be appropriate also that the offender should be required to make an apology. Should the offense be repeated, suspension would be a proper punishment. Private reproof also should be given in connection with the first offense, so as to prevent, if possible, a repetition.

11. **Usurpation of Rights.**—Trespassing upon the rights of others should be promptly reproved by the teacher. Trespassing upon the property of others may be punished in a similar manner. If injury be done to the property, whether intentional or otherwise, restitution should be made, and when the privileges of another are interfered with by a pupil he should be required to make proper apologies.

12. **False Accusation.**—Pupils frequently, in order to bring trouble upon others or escape punishment them-

selves, falsely accuse those who are innocent. The offense is a serious one, and the punishment should be prompt and effective. In all such cases it would be proper to deprive the guilty one of such school privileges as permit him to associate with his fellows. He should be made to feel that he is unworthy to be their companion. Severe private reproof, in which he should be made to understand the cowardliness of his action, would also be appropriate, and in extreme cases an apology should be made to the one who has been wronged.

13. **Defamation.**—Speaking evil of another for the purpose of injuring his character, gratifying one's propensity for gossip, or degrading another, is an offense which should be met with prompt and severe punishment. It is an offense to which the jealous and the envious are particularly prone. The teacher should do all that is possible to imbue his pupils with a feeling that this offense is cowardly and that it ought to be reprimanded wherever it is met. A pupil who speaks evil of others ought to be shut away from their society. Whenever he is detected in the offense he might be required to ask pardon of the one whom he has misrepresented or whose character he has attempted to traduce. He should be made to feel that no one but a coward speaks ill of another in his absence, and, while the teacher administers to him severe private reproof, the enormity and wickedness of his offense should also be explained to him.

14. **Speaking Evil of the School.**—It is no less wrong to slander the character of the school than it is to slander the character of an individual member of the school. A

pupil may rightfully complain to the teacher with reference to what he believes to be weakness in a school, and the teacher ought to be willing to correct the fault; but the pupil has no right to misrepresent the school, either to his schoolmates or to others. Reproof will usually correct the evil, but if the offense be continued, then suspension or expulsion must be the final resort.

15. Disrespect.—Every teacher should attempt to merit and secure the respect of his pupils. Those who strive to secure this respect by their own personal worthiness and by their kindness to the pupils usually succeed. In some cases, however, ill-disposed pupils are not won over to the teacher, and they take every opportunity to annoy him and show their disrespect for him and his authority. In such cases private reproof would probably have little effect. If reproof is desirable, it should first be given in the shape of general reproof, and if this fail, then in the shape of public reproof, that the teacher may turn the public sentiment of the school against the offender. Should all these fail, then a suspension from school privileges may be employed as the final punishment.

16. Disobedience.—This offense is of greater magnitude when willful than is that of disrespect, because it embraces not only that offense, but also the open act of defying authority.

Disobedience may be the result of thoughtlessness, and in most cases this is the true cause. Children are full of life, and we must not expect them to have the dignity and judgment of men and women. Thoughtless disobedience needs but little punishment. A simple reminder of a neglected duty or a disobedient act will promptly bring forth the child's apology, " I did not mean to do so." The teacher or the parent who punishes no further will train that child to be thoughtful and obedient, while he who administers severe reproof and finds fault, or uses any other harsh punishment, will have good prospect of succeeding in making the child hate school and grow up heedless and thoughtless of all authority.

When disobedience is willful the punishment should be severe. Where pupils openly disregard and defy authority corporal punishment is justifiable, and it may be applied if the teacher possess the necessary physical strength. When a pupil threatens to disobey, prompt measures must be taken to compel obedience. If the teacher be not strong enough to administer physical punishment, prompt suspension or dismissal from school may be resorted to as a proper punishment. Should the offender continue to annoy the school, he should be dealt with as any other outsider committing a breach of the peace, by turning him over to the officers of the law.

17. Conspiracy.—One of the most serious offenses of which pupils may be guilty is that of conspiracy. The moment a pupil enters into a conspiracy for the purpose of destroying or interfering with school authority he becomes a traitor. In all punishments for treason it is safe to adopt the maxim, " No compromise with traitors." Conspirators must be compelled to submit or leave the school. With pupils on one side plotting treason and rebellion, and teachers on the other attempting to establish and maintain authority, there ought to be no question as to the final result. Any punishment becomes justifiable at such a time, and the most severe measures are not too harsh. Boards of Directors should be prompt to respond to the appeals of the teacher and expel those who plot the downfall of the school. If, however, the conspiracy can be broken up by using corporal punishment, it is better that this should first be tried, leaving expulsion as the final punishment.

18. A General Disregard for the Good Order of the School.—Thoughtlessness on the part of pupils will always be the source of more or less disorder, and great patience is consequently demanded of the teacher. Much disorder arises, however, from a spirit of recklessness on the part of pupils, and a disregard of what is demanded of them in school. Self-enjoyment is uppermost in their minds, and this becomes the ruling motive of their actions. As a result, if they feel like talking, they talk; if they are inclined to quarrel, they quarrel; and so on.

The kinds of offenses arising under this general disregard for the order of the school are numerous. Among them are loud talking, walking heavily over the floor, calling to the teacher, making a noise with the chairs and the desk-lids, throwing books forcibly upon the desks, boisterous laughter, forced coughing, leaving the seats without permission, etc., all of which have their special modes of punishment, as heretofore suggested.

Talking pupils may be separated from the others; those who walk heavily may be put to practice in light walking; those who call to the teacher may be made to sit near him on the platform; those who are noisy at their desks may be deprived of the privilege of sitting at desks; those who throw books forcibly upon the desk may be required to pick them up again and lay them down quietly; boisterous laughter and unnecessary coughing may be quieted by a warning look from the teacher, to be followed by a subsequent private reproof; leaving the seats without permission may be punished by refusing to permit the pupil to return to his seat, directing him to the platform instead,—thus adapting the punishment in every case to the nature of the offense committed.

19. A General Disregard for Study.—Pupils who are inclined to waste time or who neglect to prepare their lessons may be punished in various ways. Among the most effective methods is that of making their class-standing depend on their progress. Those who fail to keep pace with their classmates because of idleness may be required to join a lower class. Occasionally their class-record may be read to the scholars, and the comparison be drawn between the studious and the idle, showing the comparative progress of the two kinds of pupils. Taking away the play-privileges from those who fail to do their school work is also found to be an effective mode of punishment.

20. Irregular Attendance.—When irregular attendance is the fault of the parent, as it often is, it would be unfair for the teacher to administer any punishment beyond that which Nature inflicts in the loss of position in school and class-standing. Not the child, but the parent, is the one deserving blame.

Where irregular attendance is the result of the child's

16

dislike for school or his aversion to study, the teacher should meet the difficulty by trying to make school pleasant and inviting and create in the pupil a love for study. The child is punished for irregularity of attendance, partly by his loss of class-position and partly by the greater difficulties he experiences in the study of disconnected lessons as the result of his absence from the school. In addition to these, a proper punishment would be that of putting him in lower classes as he is found to fall more and more behind his classmates.

21. **Truancy.**—This offense adds deception to irregularity of attendance. The same methods as heretofore advised should be used to induce the attendance of the child at school; but there are depraved natures which cannot be reached by even the greatest patience and kindness on the part of the teacher. Truants deceive not only teachers, but also parents. An effective means of breaking up truancy is for the teacher and the parents to work in entire harmony, the teacher reporting every absence as it occurs, and the parent reporting to the teacher every time the child is necessarily detained at home. Constant vigilance is necessary on the part of both.

Where a truant's example proves injurious to the school, and the teacher does not have the co-operation of the parent, there seems to be nothing left, if the pupil does not feel his class degradation, except suspension or expulsion. But the teacher should, before resorting to either, exhaust every other means in his power to reclaim the pupil and teach him self-respect.

CHAPTER VI.

The Teacher.

It is not necessary to argue that the teacher should be qualified for the work which his profession imposes upon him. The unqualified teacher is of course unfit for the place he occupies. It is hoped that the time is past when every one that chose could step from the position of plough-boy or sewing-girl to the teacher's desk, and without any preliminary preparation attempt to manage the school-children of a community, and instruct, guide, and direct the minds and mould the characters of ·the future citizens. The work is of too much importance to permit its being placed in the hands of the untrained and the inexperienced.

The *Teacher's Qualifications* may be said to have a fourfold character—*physical, intellectual, professional,* and *moral.*

1. The Teacher's Physical Qualifications.

1. **The Teacher should Have Good Health.**—He should, if possible, be a person of good physical development and sound constitution. Those whose nervous organization is weak, or whose health is such that they are easily unbalanced by excitement, should not think of becoming teachers. Good management and good teaching need coolness and deliberation. Dyspeptics, if in-

clined to be moody and morose or ill-natured, ought not to teach. Their example is an unsafe one for children to imitate, and for the sake of their own health as well as that of their pupils they should engage in work of a different character.

2. The Teacher should be a Person of Good Hygienic Habits.—It is not enough that he enter upon his work with good health; it is necessary also that he preserve his health by giving due attention to hygienic laws. The person who takes upon himself the work of the school-room will find that his duties are by no means light, and that constant watchfulness is needed in order that the physical system may not be caused to suffer.

The teacher must give heed to the following hygienic *suggestions:*

1. He must give due attention to the ventilation of the school-room, that the air may be as pure as possible.

2. He must take sufficient exercise in the open air, that his blood may be made pure and life-sustaining.

3. He must eat healthful, nutritious food, and enough of it to satisfy the demands of health.

4. He must take sufficient sleep and at regular times.

5. He must alternate work with recreation, that the mind as well as the body may have its proper degree of rest.

6. He must avoid the use of stimulants as a beverage, also narcotics; the teacher needs a clear brain.

7. He must give due attention to his clothing, that the temperature of his body may vary as little as possible.

8. He must give proper attention to light when engaged in study, that his sight may be preserved uninjured.

9. He must preserve an even temper, that the noise and worry of the school may not cause undue nervous excitement and exhaustion.

10. He must give proper attention to bathing, that the skin may be kept in a healthy condition.

11. He must give attention to social culture, both for relaxation of mind and for the good it will do him to become better acquainted with the community.

12. He must take regular physical exercise of some kind, that his muscles may become strengthened, his brain be kept clear, and his physical constitution remain vigorous.

2. The Teacher's Intellectual Qualifications.

1. **His Scholarship should be Thorough.**—The teacher should feel that he has mastered the branches he attempts to teach. A knowledge of the textbook in use and its contents is not enough. He should know what other textbooks contain, and in addition to this much that is not to be found in textbooks. To illustrate, his knowledge of the geography of a country must be broader than is given in any textbook. Cyclopædias, gazetteers, newspapers, etc. should be consulted, that he may have a fund of knowledge with which to illustrate and add to the textbook matter.

2. **His Knowledge should be Broad and General.**—All knowledge gives culture. The teacher whose knowledge extends beyond the branches he attempts to teach will be more successful than he who knows only what he attempts to impart to others. The teacher whose knowledge includes Algebra and Geometry will teach Arithmetic better than one whose knowledge of mathematics

is limited to Arithmetic alone. Thus, also, one will teach Reading much better by having a thorough knowledge of Grammar, Rhetoric, and Etymology, or Geography better from a knowledge of History, Geology, and Mineralogy. Each study helps to broaden our knowledge of the others. The broader and the more extensive the knowledge of the teacher the better the work he will be enabled to accomplish.

3. **His Knowledge should be Accurate.**—Pupils repose little confidence in the teacher whose knowledge is frequently found to be inaccurate, and their confidence in him will be still less if he is unwilling to acknowledge a mistake when he is found to be in error. It is a hard thing to acknowledge a mistake, but the teacher should not hesitate for a moment to correct himself or admit the error when his attention is called to it by the pupil. It would be much better, of course, if he were to make no errors. Should he find himself unable to answer a question, he should be candid enough to say so frankly, or offer to search out the answer for the pupil.

4. **He should Keep Pace with Current History.**—The teacher who does not keep up with the progress of the times necessarily retrogrades. No one should have a more thorough knowledge of what is taking place at present than the teacher. He needs this knowledge to awaken interest, to illustrate, and to adapt his teaching to the times in which he lives. This knowledge must be not only of the current events of his own national history, but also of other countries and nations. The teacher must be a politician in the sense that he must know thoroughly the history, both past and present, of his own country.

5. **He must Have a Well-disciplined Mind.**—Discipline is the chief end of education. The teacher who hopes to train the minds of others and impart mental discipline must himself possess a mind well disciplined. The teacher must be a clear, logical thinker. Every thought must be well defined. His knowledge must not be a mass of disconnected facts and details, but well classified and systematized as a whole. One whose knowledge consists of disintegrated fragments is hardly prepared to give systematic training to the minds of others. The teacher's knowledge should be so methodically arranged in his mind that he may have it always at command.

6. **His Knowledge should be Available.**—A lack of mental discipline makes one's knowledge unavailable. We may pursue our studies in such a way as to gather a great number of facts, and yet have none at command when most needed. The teacher should be able to tell what he knows, and tell it in such a way as to attract and interest his pupils. He must necessarily be able to put his thoughts in good language also, not only that his pupils may understand, but also that they may find his manner of expression such as is worthy of imitation. Ability to communicate our ideas readily and understandingly is one of the essentials of successful teaching.

7. **He should Have a Knowledge of the Human Mind.**— A knowledge of the mental faculties and their mode of operation is of great benefit to every one who in any sense finds it necessary to influence the minds of others. In this respect the teacher and the orator find themselves on a common level. But in addition to this the teacher must know the relative order of development of these faculties and the best methods of culture. The order

of studies and the methods of teaching each individual study must be harmonized with the order of mental development. To attempt to teach subjects which require highly-developed reasoning powers at an age when the child's reasoning faculties are yet undeveloped would be not only useless, but also mischievous. The teacher must be a student of psychology at least to such an extent as will enable him to understand the operation of the various mental powers, their order of development, their proper methods of culture, and the studies best adapted to the culture of each.

8. He should Have a Thorough Knowledge of the Human Body.—A knowledge of Human Physiology and Hygiene is essential to every teacher, not only that he may know how best to preserve his own health, but also that he may know how to give the best physical training to his pupils and care for their health and comfort. The physical welfare of both pupils and teacher is quite as important as their mental welfare, and no less preparation should be made to promote the one than to promote the other. It would be well for every teacher were he required to pass an examination in Physiology and Hygiene before being permitted to enter the school-room as a teacher. This knowledge would aid him greatly also in understanding the causes of disorder, and thus enable him to manage the school more successfully.

3. The Teacher's Professional Qualifications.

Teaching is a science. Its principles are readily determined and reduced to a system. Like most other sciences, it is empirical. Its principles are the result of observation and experience. *School Management* and

Methods of Culture and Instruction embrace the principles of this science, and they may of course be taught to those preparing for the work of teaching. This is properly the work of Normal Schools and Teachers' Institutes. But no agency can implant in any mind those elements of character which are essential to success in this calling.

Aptness to Teach is the first great requisite to success. Teachers are born, not made. Normal Schools may develop latent talent, but they cannot change or displace the elements of character which Nature has implanted in the human mind. No medical school can make a skillful surgeon of one who is awkward, however well it may teach the anatomy of the human body or deftly explain the principles underlying skillful surgical practice; nor can it make a kind, sympathizing physician of an uncouth and brutal man. All it can do, and all any professional school can pretend to do, is to develop and train that latent power with which Nature may have endowed the individual. It is the business of the Normal School to acquaint its students with the best methods of teaching, culture, discipline, and all else that concerns the great work in which they are to engage, but to pretend to make expert teachers and disciplinarians of those who by Nature are deprived of that aptness for teaching and discipline which characterizes all successful teachers, would be mere quackery.

This aptness or special fitness to teach embraces a number of professional qualifications, each of which is more or less important.

1. **The Teacher should be Able to Manage Well.**—Inability to manage a school is in most cases the chief

source of failure. The teacher needs a thorough knowledge of human nature. He must be ingenious, wide awake, energetic, cool-headed, and have the skill necessary to adapt means to ends. He must be a constant student of child mind and character. He should acquaint himself with the children's whims and caprices. He ought to examine carefully into the experience of others, and wisely shape his own work by their success or failure. He should also study carefully the principles of management, and modify them in his own practice to suit the circumstances of each particular case.

The teacher needs tact. Child-nature is but human nature, and it is much the same throughout the civilized world. The teacher should study the art of management thoroughly, and then have the tact necessary to adapt his methods to the control of every case that may arise. No man can less afford to enter upon his work without this preliminary training than can the teacher.

2. **The Teacher should Have a Full Knowledge of his Work.**—He must understand fully the objects of education. He must understand not only the human mind, but also how to give it proper culture. He should understand the capacities of the mind, and have definite ends in view as to its training. He must understand that the child is not a mere receiver into which he can pour all sorts of knowledge, but rather that it is a being capable of almost unlimited culture, and that his mission is not to impart knowledge so much as it is to place the child in such a favorable position as will enable it to gain knowledge by its own efforts.

3. **The Teacher should be Acquainted with the Best Methods of Teaching.**—It is a grave error to think that

any one of good education can teach well. Teaching is a profession in itself. Many years of experience have developed new and valuable methods of imparting instruction, and the most successful teacher is he that keeps pace with the progress of his profession in adopting as his own what he finds valuable in all methods. The approved methods of the present represent the thought, culture, and experience of centuries. The presentation of a subject to the minds of children is no longer a haphazard proceeding, but it is governed instead by methods which have been fully tested and which are based on well-fixed principles.

In addition to a knowledge of these methods the teacher must have skillful practice. The beginner cannot expect to succeed as does the one who has been practicing correct methods for a series of years. Practice and experience give one faith and confidence in his work. It is only continued practice that brings great skill.

4. The Teacher should Have a Thorough Knowledge of Educational Means.—He should understand the wants of every individual child. He should not only know when to punish, but also what punishment to inflict. He should know not only what branches ought to be taught to the child, but also when they should be taught. He should know not only in what order the mental powers are developed, but also what studies are best suited to aid in that development. He should know not only how to instruct, but also how to train, and how to use the means in his power to accomplish the desired end.

5. He should Have the Ability to Impart Instruction in an Interesting Manner.—The interesting teacher is always

the successful teacher. He is also the teacher who at-tracts pupils to his school, and keeps them there. A child that is interested never fails to love school and to learn. The teacher, too, who succeeds in interesting his pupils finds little to do in the matter of government or management. Indeed, interested pupils find little time to be mischievous or disorderly. An interesting teacher is therefore usually also a good disciplinarian as well as a good instructor.

6. The Teacher must be a Wise Legislator.—It will fall to his lot to make many of the regulations by which the school shall be controlled. These regulations should be such as will win the approbation not only of the children, but also of the community. It will often be found to be the case that the teacher can secure the assent of the pu-pils in the adoption of such regulations as may be judicious and necessary. Great wisdom is needed in the adoption of rules, that they be such only as are found necessary for the best interests of the school. All other rules are mischievous and calculated to do more harm than good.

7. The Teacher should be an Efficient Executive.—He must not only know how to make wise rules, but also how to enforce them wisely and impartially. The teacher must have no favorites when it comes to enforcing rules or administering discipline. His judgment should be clear and unbiased. He should look on all sides of an offense. He should clearly understand what motive prompted the offender, and if punishment be found necessary he should administer it impartially. Order should be preserved, but it were better that ninety-nine guilty should escape rather than that one innocent pupil should be unwisely or unjustly punished. The teacher ought to make no mistakes in this direction.

The teacher must be efficient, not only in liscipline, but also in the entire management of the school. Classes should be promptly called and promptly dismissed, questions should be put promptly, and prompt answers should be required in return. All the school work should be done in good order and at the proper time. The teacher needs to be wide awake, prompt, and self-possessed at all times. A school under the guidance of an efficient executive approaches as nearly as possible to self-government.

8. He should be Interested in the Advancement of his Profession.—Teachers cannot afford to ignore the profession which they represent. They should rather be active to assist in building it up. They should attend Teachers' Institutes and Conventions, and assist in making them practical and instructive. They should watch carefully the progress of educational events, read educational journals, and, whenever possible, contribute to the columns of these journals anything they may have found of value in their own experience. They should contend for the rights of their profession, and show its importance to those who attempt to throw ridicule upon it. They should advocate professional training for this calling as for any other, but not at the expense of the children, as is necessarily the case where a young teacher enters the school-room without training, and practices on the pupils for many years until he acquires by experience what he might have learned in a year or two by the careful study of educational handbooks or received by training and instruction at a well-conducted Normal School.

9. The Teacher should be Progressive—He must be a

close student, keeping up with the times not only in his knowledge of current history, but also in that which most closely concerns his own profession. He should visit the schools of other teachers, and be a close observer of their methods of instruction and management. He should constantly strive for professional improvement. He should not rest satisfied with knowing that he is esteemed a good teacher, but earnestly strive to become as good as the best. He should not condemn new methods, but carefully examine them and weigh their merits, and, if he find them good, adopt them, unless he already has a better.

10. **The Teacher should be Liberal in his Views.**—He should give the widest latitude to the thoughts of others. He should not bind himself to any one method, and insist upon that as being the only correct method. Radicalism in education is fanaticism of the narrowest type. The liberal-minded teacher never rides hobbies, but, on the other hand, sees good in what others do as well as in what he himself does. The liberal teacher does not condemn new methods because they are new, nor, on the other hand, does he adopt them because of their novelty. He considers their merits and demerits, tests them in practice, judges of their results, and adopts or rejects as he deems most wise.

4. The Teacher's Moral Qualifications.

Among the chief moral qualifications which should characterize the good teacher are the following:

1. **He should be a Good Man.**—The example of the teacher is powerful in moulding the character of the young. The teacher's moral character and his conduct should be entirely above reproach. He should be a

model that his pupils may imitate with profit. Not only his teachings, but also his conduct, should be such as to win the approbation of the community. He need not be sanctimonious and solemn—indeed, he should not be, for such traits of moral character are repulsive to children—but his virtues should be of such a positive nature as to guide his pupils aright without even the aid of moral teachings.

2. He should be Impartial.—No one more nearly fills the position of legislator and judge in one than does the teacher. He not only makes his own laws, but he also expounds and executes them. Should he be partial in his treatment of pupils or in the application of his laws, the injustice will be detected at once by those who suffer. In his judgments he must show no favoritism. All his pupils, whether rich or poor, high or low, bright or stupid, should have the same rights and privileges. He is not, indeed, called upon to love all alike, but he must be impartial to all, unless some have by their conduct forfeited all claims to respect; but even in such cases kind and impartial treatment will frequently reclaim those who have been given up as lost.

3. He should be Friendly to Children.—Friendship is a motive-power which influences all of us, and leads us to do our work better than we would in its absence. We do those things cheerfully for our friends which otherwise we would leave undone or do only under a pressing sense of duty. This rule holds also with children. For those who have a kind word of commendation and for those whom they regard as their friends they are ever ready to be obedient and obliging. The teacher who can lead his pupils to feel that he is their friend, and that every-

thing he does is for their welfare, has reduced the difficulties of discipline to the minimum. But, independent of the advantages which the teacher reaps from his being friendly to children, it is one of his plain moral duties to be friendly to all those who are placed in his charge. It is not enough that he treat them impartially; it is not enough that he be a good man. Many a good man, so far as worldly judgment goes, is strictly impartial and just, but at the same time austere, sullen, morose, and inclined to weigh in the balance every act of childhood strictly according to justice, without showing any disposition to be either merciful, kind, or generous.

The teacher whom the children regard as their friend wields an influence in moulding character whose power can scarcely be estimated. It was this which in a great measure gave to Dr. Arnold almost unlimited power and influence at Rugby; and it is this which in every case, from the primary school to the university, brings to the side of the teacher those warm advocates and adherents who in both act and speech are ever ready to do battle for his good name and the work on which his reputation. is based.

4. **The Teacher should Love Children.**—The man or the woman who has no love for children, no sympathy with childhood, no disposition to overlook·the little frailties which have characterized children ever since the creation of the race, ought to have no place in the school-room. If there are persons who are totally and absolutely unfit for the position of teacher, they are the men who have no love for children, and no disposition to overlook and excuse the shortcomings and the thoughtlessness of wayward childish impulses.

As has been said heretofore, no teacher probably will have the same degree of affection for all the pupils of his school. This is hardly possible, for the personal character of pupils differs greatly, and we find the varying shades of character from amiability to selfishness so distinct, and some faults so positive, that, in the nature of things, while the teacher may love all, there are some for whom his affection will be more marked than for others. And yet even in such cases his love may prove all-powerful in guiding and directing them aright.

5. The Teacher should be an Agreeable Companion.— Few teachers wield so great an influence over their school as do they who try to make themselves agreeable, pleasant, and sociable with their pupils. The child who feels that he can approach his teacher and have a social talk with him, or now and then relate a story or enjoy a joke in his presence, is ready at all times to defend that teacher, and he will at the same time hold him in the very highest regard.

This pleasantness of manner should manifest itself also in the recitation. Of course the object of the recitation is work, but if that work can be done in an agreeable and pleasant manner by both teacher and pupils, it will be all the better. If the teacher can occasionally relate an amusing anecdote which will serve to create interest while it also amuses, let him do so. A good laugh in class, or indeed a good laugh in which the whole school may join, will be quite as beneficial as if the time were employed in hard study.

The teacher ought to be cheerful at all times, though he should never be undignified, for clownishness does not become a teacher. In the recitation he should be bright, lively, and sparkling, and at recess or out of school he should have a cheerful word for every one he meets. He should let the pupils feel that he is interested in their sports and that he enjoys their plays with them. Indeed, if his discipline be such that his pupils thoroughly respect him, it will be entirely appropriate for him to join in their plays, and thus heighten the children's enjoyment.

Even in the matter of refusing requests, the teacher may do it in such a way that the pupil will thoroughly respect him and see all the more clearly the necessity for the refusal. The same is true in administering punishment. If the pupil see that the teacher administers punishment reluctantly, and with as little austerity as possible, he will respect that teacher all the more and acknowledge the justice of the penalty. But if the teacher be gruff, and show by his manner that he is spiteful, vindictive, and revengeful, the pupil at once loses respect for him, and the chief ends of punishment are defeated.

It is a serious mistake to suppose that because a teacher calls attention to a fault good-naturedly the pupil gives no heed to the reproof. Scolding accomplishes little at any time, and in the end it simply makes the teacher ridiculous, while it loses all possible good effect on the pupil. It is a common subject of remark with reference to a cross teacher, "Oh, you must get used to his scolding; it does not mean anything." What shall be said, however, of discipline which pupils seek to extenuate in order to excuse a teacher's weakness of character? Good-natured reproof, on the other hand, is much the more effective, and it also preserves the pupil's respect for the discipline and personal fitness of the teacher.

6. **The Teacher should be Neat in Person.**—"Cleanliness is next to godliness." One of the teacher's physical qualifications is that *he should be a person of good hygienic habits.* This is also to some extent a moral qualification. The personal habits of the teacher will be copied by his pupils, and this is true not only of his habits, but also of his manner of dress. Let him be untidy and slovenly, and his pupils will follow his example. Let him be careful to keep his desk, his person, and his clothing clean and neat, and without a word of instruction one after another the pupils will acquire the habit of neatness.

His influence is either for good or for evil; and this being true, it is not only expedient, but it becomes also a positive moral duty, for him to set such an example in both his dress and his manner as will be profitable for his pupils to imitate.

7. **The Teacher should be Honest and Truthful.**—It seems hardly necessary to argue the importance of this moral qualification of teachers, and yet so many are untruthful and dishonest in a certain sense that it becomes a matter of serious import. It is necessary that the teacher be honest and truthful—

1. *To Himself.*—He has no right to overwork himself and destroy his health in his enthusiasm and anxiety to win a reputation or in his desire to succeed and make a good impression on the community. His effort to do good is laudable, but the claims of society and the claims of his own health must not be ignored.

2. *To His Pupils.*—Independent of the culture and instruction which the teacher owes to his pupils, it is his duty to be truthful and candid in telling them their

faults when such a course becomes necessary. It is both wise and proper that he encourage them, but I e ought not to encourage in such a way as to leave the pupils under the impression that the work they are doing is good and satisfactory when the reverse of this is the truth.

He must be honest in his work with them, doing all for them that it is their right to expect. He must be truth ful as to his ability also in the matter of overcoming dif-ficulties. He has no right to answer questions at random, and then, when he finds himself in error, attempt to con-ceal it by passing on hastily to something else or by assuming that it is impertinent for his pupils to doubt his statements. The teacher has no right to be untruth-ful by design, and when he finds himself wrong uninten-tionally it is but right to make the proper correction at once.

3. *To His Patrons.*—The teacher has no right to de-ceive his patrons by telling them falsehoods as to the progress of their children. It is much easier to say a good word of every child, however dull, than to state the exact truth to the parent. But the parent is rarely deceived by a false statement. No one knows the weak points and the shortcomings of a child better than does the parent. A false statement with reference to a child's progress, therefore, simply leads the patron to believe the teacher untruthful and dishonest.

8. **The Teacher should be Modest.**—Especially should he be modest with reference to telling of what he has ac-complished. If he be a progressive and energetic teacher who has done much good in a district, there will always be many who will gladly speak words of praise in his favor. Many, of course, will be envious and seek every

occasion to misrepresent him and his work. So long as cynics and gossips exist we must expect them to find fault, but it is not the good opinion of these that the wise teacher seeks to win, and he need give them no attention. Modesty will win friends for him among those whose friendship is worth having, where a spirit of boastfulness would tend to estrange and disgust them.

9. **The Teacher should be Industrious and Faithful.**—This is a requisite of success in every calling. The industrious teacher who is faithful to his employers and the interests of his school need have little fear of failure, unless, indeed, there be some very grave defects in other essential requisites of character. Lazy teachers ought never to be employed. The work of teaching needs energy, industry, and tact such as is not found in a man who is indolent. In addition to this, the example of a lazy teacher is pernicious in making the pupils careless and idle.

10. **The Teacher should be Conscientious.**—This requisite or qualification of the teacher embraces many of his other moral qualifications, for a conscientious man will under all circumstances strive to do his duty. A conscientious teacher will do his duty not only to his pupils, but also to the patrons and school officers of the district. He will be careful also to see that the school property is well preserved. He will look well to the health as well as to the progress of his pupils—to their physical and their moral welfare as well as to their intellectual wants. He will see to it that the governing principle which rules himself as well as the school is the desire to do right at all times, and this principle will guide and direct him in all

his work both while in the school-room ard while engaged in cultivating an educational sentiment in the community.

5. Faults to be Avoided by Teachers.

There are few teachers who approximate perfection in the matter of *School Management.* Even the best often find themselves unconsciously making mistakes which to some extent interfere with their progress and success. Many of these mistakes may, with proper forethought and caution, be avoided. The chief of them are named in the following pages. Young teachers particularly should give them careful consideration and avoid them whenever possible.

1. Hobby-Riding.—The teacher may have hobbies either in *Management* or in *Methods of Instruction.* Both are alike objectionable, and both indicate a narrowness of mind which ought not to be characteristic of a teacher. Liberal-minded men are not given to the riding of hobbies.

In Government the hobby-rider is either a strict advocate of the old-time corporal punishment, to be administered in such a way as will cause the culprit to keep it in lively remembrance, or he is an advocate of moral suasion, who believes that under no circumstances should a child ever be subjected to physical punishment. There is no middle ground for the hobby-rider; he must gravitate from one extreme to the other.

In Methods the hobby-rider drifts rapidly from one to another, being an advocate of each in turn. First he advocates no oral instruction, and, failing here, flies immediately to the opposite extreme, and insists on it that neither the teacher nor the pupil shall have anything to do with textbooks. At one time he devotes the greater part of his attention to oral spelling; suddenly he is converted to a new method, and from that time forward all recitations must be conducted in writing. For a while his hobby is oral arithmetic, and he regards the great object of it as being the ability to solve all the puzzling questions of some textbook on that branch; then he becomes an ardent advocate of the policy of discarding oral arithmetic entirely and solving problems by the written process alone. For a while his hobby is object lessons, then it is oral instruction, then language lessons, then the spelling reform; and thus from one to another, never stopping long enough to inquire into the merits of any of his hobbies, but ever deserting the old for the new.

Teachers should have no hobbies; they should inquire narrowly into the merits of all methods, and, having wisely made their choice, steadily adhere to it until convinced that something more valuable is within their reach.

2. Adhering too Closely to Textbooks.—Textbooks are meant to be an aid only, and the teacher should not insist that the words of any book be memorized. Herbert Spencer says, "The function of books is supplementary —a means of seeing through other men's eyes what you cannot see for yourself." The facts and the principles are the important things to know, not the exact words in which they are stated. I remember distinctly hearing in my boyhood the following question and answer:

Teacher. Why does blowing upon hot coffee make it cooler?

Pupil Because the breath is cooler than the coffee,

and the temperature of the two tends to become equalized.

But the teacher was not satisfied with this original and correct answer; it was not the answer of the text-book; so the question was passed to the next pupil, who informed the class that it was because the peculiar shape of the mouth in blowing made the breath cooler. The boy who gave the first answer lost his faith in that teacher, and he had but little respect for his ability ever after.

Teacher, if a pupil give you a correct answer in his own language, accept it without question, though it be neither so elegant nor so concisely expressed as it is in the textbook. Show your pupils how to get the sense, the meaning, out of the printed page. They can read the words for themselves, but sometimes they do not know how to use the textbook to the best advantage.

3. Teaching Words instead of Ideas.—This is one of the chief errors of inexperienced teachers. Pupils should understand what they attempt to learn. The mere memorizing of page after page without comprehension trains but one faculty of the mind, and that in a way and to an extent not to be commended. A single idea awakened in the mind of the child by a skillful and suggestive teacher is worth more than a week's memorizing. It is the business of the teacher to arouse thought, to develop mind, to put the child in such a state that he may gain knowledge and training by his own effort, and not to crowd the mind and tax the memory with a collection of meaningless words.

4. Too Much Memorizing.—The tendency under the older forms and methods of education was to train the

memory almost wholly at the expense and to the neglect
of the other faculties. This was to some extent the result of the deficiency of books and printing. Libraries
were scarce, and even after the invention of printing the
price of books was so high that only the wealthy could
indulge in the luxury of reading. Newspapers had not
been introduced. As a consequence, the memory was
cultured to a much greater extent than at present, and
courses of study were arranged accordingly. In later
years we still have adhered somewhat to the old methods,
possibly because of the fact that the memory is that
power by which we are best able to make a display of
our knowledge. The best methods of culture train the
mental powers symmetrically, giving the memory its
due share of training, but not at the expense of the observing powers or any of the other mental faculties.

5. Educational Cramming.—The enthusiastic teacher is
anxious usually to do more in the way of imparting
knowledge than is really beneficial to the child. Sometimes also this educational cramming is the result of a
forced preparation for examination. Lessons are often
too long; too much haste is made to finish a book; too
many studies are undertaken; and often certain branches
are taught at too early an age. Sometimes parents urge
upon the teacher the importance of spurring on the
children. The teacher is assured that the children have
plenty of spare time in the evening, and that it would
be better if they had more study to engage their attention at that time. The teacher becomes anxious, and
feels that he ought to require more work of the pupils,
and he therefore lengthens the lessons or adds more
studies to the schedule; and the final result is a super-

ficial knowledge of many things, and no thorough knowledge of the principles of any study.

This cramming also partakes of the nature of useless
facts and details which we attempt to force into the minds
of our pupils. As a result, useful knowledge is sacrificed,
mental training is ignored, and the chief ends of education are defeated in our effort to furnish our children
with knowledge and make them living cyclopædias.

We should not attempt to train the faculties nor impart knowledge more rapidly than the mental growth
and development of the learner will permit. The
growth of the child's mind must be a healthy growth if
we desire to have the mind healthy in after life.

6. Attempting to Teach Too Much.—The teacher should
not attempt to teach his pupils all that he himself knows.
Much must be left untaught. Pupils learn but slowly.
Their minds develop in accordance with fixed laws, and
normal growth cannot be judiciously hastened. The
teacher must therefore not hurry them, nor be discouraged because they do not seem to progress as rapidly as
he might desire. The number of studies for all grades,
but particularly for the younger pupils, should be limited to a few, at most four or five.

Many things which to the teacher seem easy are to the
pupils extremely difficult. The teacher should therefore
not confuse his pupils by suggesting various ways of
overcoming a difficulty until he first sees that they thoroughly comprehend a single one. Many a pupil has
been heartily discouraged because his teacher, in his anxiety to help the pupil out of difficulty, has simply confused him by attempting to teach too many things at
once, or by attempting to teach too many ways of se-

curing a result before the pupil had thoroughly comprehended any one way.

7. Striving after the Impossible.—Nature has fixed certain limits in the character of every mind, beyond which it is useless for the teacher to attempt to reach. All the hurry and worry of the teacher cannot push a child beyond its capacity. There will always be dull pupils whom no teacher can brighten, there will always be slow ones whose development no teacher can hasten. It is a waste of time to attempt to accomplish what is impossible. The bright pupils, the prodigies, are the exception, but the teacher's work with the dull, the thoughtless, and the careless is not therefore less valuable or less productive of good results.

Quaint old Thomas Fuller gave this excellent advice two centuries ago: " Wines, the stronger they be, the more lees they have when they are new. Many boys are muddy-headed till they be clarified with age; and such afterward proved the best. Bristol diamonds are both bright and square and pointed by Nature, and yet are soft and worthless; whereas Orient ones in India are rough and rugged naturally. Hard, rugged, and dull natures in youth acquit themselves afterward the jewels of the country; and therefore their dullness at first is to be borne with, if they be diligent. The schoolmaster deserves to be beaten himself who beats Nature in a boy for a fault. And I question whether all the whipping in the world can make their parts who are naturally sluggish rise one minute before the hour Nature hath appointed. All the whetting in the world can never set a razor's edge on that which hath no steel in it."

8. Suppressing Originality and Individuality.—One of

the greatest errors in teaching is that of trying to east all in the same mould. Over-systematic teachers make the mistake of insisting that all the members of a class must be proficient in every branch they attempt to study. The student should never be judged by his ability in all branches, but rather on his average ability. There are those to whom mathematics will always be distasteful, and whose knowledge in that science must ever be largely a matter of memory. There are others, again, who have a great capacity for mathematics, but whose talents for language and natural science are but mediocre. To suppress these individual tastes, to attempt to mould anew these minds, to try to bring them to an artificial and arbitrary standard or course of study, and insist that each shall be proficient in all, and that individual preference and individual talent shall not be permitted to assert themselves, is to destroy individuality itself.

Under our present school system of course all the teacher can attempt to do is to give general instruction. It is not his business, nor is it the business of the public school, to make specialists. Special training is the work of the *technical schools.* But, while his efforts should be directed wholly in the line of giving this general knowledge and this general culture which our school system contemplates, the originality which a child displays should not be discouraged, nor should the individuality which distinguishes each one from every other be suppressed. It is, in reality, the men of original genius and striking personality that rise to distinction and become our leaders. The great work of the teacher consists in leading, developing, and wisely directing genius, rather than in curbing and suppressing the efforts of individual talent.

9. Making the Chief Work of School the Mastery of Textbooks.—Textbooks are valuable in presenting the salient points of a study, in systematizing the work of teaching, and in directing the learner to the proper method of developing the branches of which they treat; but the teacher must not make the mistake of supposing that when the textbook is mastered by his pupils they are proficient in the branch of which it treats. The mastery of textbooks is not the object of school work, and yet there are probably few of us who were not taught in our school-days to believe that the great aim was to finish the books and be able to pass a creditable examination. Indeed, the same fault exists to-day in all except the very best schools. Discipline, training, and all other ends of study are forgotten in the effort to solve problems, demonstrate propositions, commit definitions, and acquire a fluent use of textbook language.

Many a boy considers his school work finished the day he closes the book with the feeling that he has mastered its contents. Very many have discovered their mistake too late in life, when they have come to apply their powers to the actual work of the world, and have found their textbook knowledge and textbook ability of use only in the school-room and in the study of special books. Under no circumstances should they be allowed to imbibe the notion that the knowledge of any one book is all that they ought to possess. They should be made to feel instead that a knowledge of principles is the great requisite, and such a knowledge of principles as will enable them to make the proper application in actual work.

10. **Being Servile Imitators.**—This fault arises largely from the lack of preparation for the work of teaching. Young men and women without the professional training necessary to engage in the work of teaching are likely to take it for granted that the ways of their own teachers are best, and they therefore imitate, and too often without the necessary tact to adapt their methods to the requirements of the case.

It is a fault particularly liable to characterize the High-School graduate, where no normal or training class exists, or where no educational works are read and studied. It is also one of the chief sources of failure, because High-School methods of both management and instruction differ widely from the methods to be employed in the Primary School, where the young and inexperienced teachers, unfortunately, are usually em ployed.

The chief means of avoiding this error lies in the preparation which every one ought to make before en tering upon the work of teaching. Not only a course of professional study is advisable, but also close observation of the work of many successful teachers and considerable preliminary practice under the eye of an expert. Our elementary schools ought not to be practice and experimental schools merely, in which the non-professional teacher may gain experience, learn methods, and earn a living at the same time.

The patience of our American people is great, and nowhere is it more pointedly exemplified than in the constant employment of an army of raw recruits who enter our schools, many of them being persons who are absolutely innocent of any knowledge of the first principles on which the science of teaching is based. To the employment of these undisciplined and non-professionally educated persons is due in a great degree also the low salaries of which teachers themselves complain so bitterly. The only remedy for both evils is the careful preparation of teachers for their work before they take up the profession.

11. Adhering to Old Methods.—Old methods that are good and which aid correct mental development should not be given up ; but, on the other hand, those which have proven non-conducive to the requirements of mental growth ought to be discarded. The adherence to old methods is not so often conservatism as it is stubbornness and the result of ignorance. The teacher who holds to a method because he knows of no better is of course right so far as his knowledge goes, but he is not fit to be a teacher if he is non-progressive or makes no attempts to learn a better way.

Swett, in his *Methods of Teaching,* gives this admirable picture of one who adheres strictly to old methods: " In arithmetic he begins with definitions, continues in abstractions and mechanical rules, and ends in puzzling problems. In grammar he omits the actual use of language in expressing thought, and devotes his attention to the technicalities of parsing and analysis. In geography he is content to have his pupils memorize regardless of ideas. In history he strings dates like wooden beads upon the thread of memory. In reading he trains pupils to call words without much reference to meaning. In botany he takes books before flowers, and in physics omits experiments. Object-lessons he regards with disdain. In fact, he does not educate at all ; that is, he does not awaken curiosity nor excite inquiry nor develop discrimination."

12. Believing that Persons can Teach Well without Preparation.—There are still many outside of the teachers' ranks, and not a few within, who think it possible for any one to teach well without special preparation. Of those engaged in teaching who believe this to be true there are very few, indeed, who are successful teachers in the true sense. They may set tasks and see them performed, they may assign lessons and hear them recited, but they do not teach except in an irregular way; neither do they secure that harmonious development of the child-mind which is a part of the work of every teacher.

Carlyle paints their picture graphically in the following words: " My teachers were hide-bound pedants, without knowledge of man's nature, or of boys, or of aught save lexicons. Innumerable dead vocables they crammed into us, and called it fostering the growth of the mind. How can an inanimate mechanical verb-grinder foster the growth of *anything*, much more of mind, which grows, not like a vegetable by having its roots littered by etymological compost, but, like a spirit, by mysterious contact with spirit-thought kindling itself at the fire of living thought? How shall he give kindling in whose own inward man there is no live coal but is burned out to a dead grammatical cinder? My professors knew syntax enough, and of the human soul this much—that it had a faculty called memory, and could be acted on through the muscular integument by the appliance of birch-rods."

Many men and women, after constant practice and

without previous preparation, learn to teach, some of them well, some passably, and some otherwise; but who shall reckon the fearful cost of all this preliminary work? Who shall be able to count up the failures and the schools spoiled? Who shall be able to estimate the damage done to both mind and morals of the young who are the innocent victims of an apprenticeship of this kind?

13. Being Non-Progressive.—No teacher ought to be willing to fall behind his associates. But in educational matters he must go either backward or forward; there can be no standing still. Too many teachers, when they have once secured a diploma or a life-certificate, are satisfied to make no further progress. This should not be the case. They ought continually to grow better. They ought to be close observers of the methods of others. They ought to be thinkers. They ought to pursue a course of educational reading. They ought to keep themselves well versed in the improvements in textbooks. If they feel that they can learn nothing at Teachers' Associations, they ought at least to be willing to do good to others by giving advice, by pointing out errors, and by encouraging the inexperienced. The teacher's calling ought to be progressive, and it should be a source of pride, particularly to every professional teacher, to promote its interests wherever possible.

14. Overwork.—The teacher's first duty is to take care of his health. Without good health he can have little success in teaching; but, independent of this, he is not called upon to sacrifice his health in order to do good work for his pupils. There is no adequate reason why a teacher may not so arrange his work as to do full jus-

tice to his pupils, and yet have plenty of time for exercise and social recreation. Sooner or later, every one must pay the penalty for infringing Nature's laws in doing more work, either physical or mental, than is compatible with the welfare of the human constitution.

When the teacher leaves the school-room he should leave his school cares and anxieties behind, and feel that he is free to engage in such recreation as is most pleasing or most beneficial. When vacation comes let him go to the woods or the mountains or the seashore, whichever is most congenial to his tastes or whichever he feels that he can best afford, and here let him throw aside all cares and enjoy Nature to the utmost.

15. **Striving to Please Everybody.**—However well the teacher may do his work, he will find many critics who feel called upon to make unpleasant criticism and find fault. Let him not be discouraged at this. No one has always escaped criticism. Were one's school absolutely perfect, he would still find some whose envy would incite them to make malicious remarks with regard to his success. Indeed, the more successful a teacher is in building up a school, and the more nearly he brings it to perfection, the greater will be the envy of his competitors, and the more energetic they will be in their efforts to say unkind and untruthful things of him and his work. It ought not so to be, but human nature is both vain and weak.

Let the teacher feel that he is doing his duty to himself and his patrons, that he is doing the best he can with the material and the opportunities at command, and he does well. He should not sacrifice the pupils in his charge in order that his school may enjoy a brilliant record and thus be the pride of the community. Popular opinion is desirable, and the good opinion of all is not to be lightly regarded, but if this good opinion must be secured as the result of injury to either pupils or teacher, the price to be paid is too high.

16. Neglecting the Practical.—The teacher should not confine his instruction to the actual school studies. The student that leaves school knowing only what concerns his textbook studies knows comparatively little. The teacher has many opportunities for imparting valuable practical knowledge, which ought not to pass without an effort to improve them. Many valuable hints may be given to the girls, and even to the boys, on the subject of domestic economy. Many homes are unhomelike because of the ignorance of those who preside over them. The good managers of homes are probably the exception, but the condition of things might be much improved if teachers were careful to make suggestions to their pupils on topics of this kind. Let the teacher read extensively on the subject of domestic economy, and then give short talks every week on the most important parts of the study. If such practice among teachers were to become general, we should have a most powerful lever in elevating the condition of the homes in our land.

The teacher should also make his instruction practical as concerns the work of the boys. Let him instill into their minds a respect for labor by showing that all of us labor in our respective spheres; that labor is not only beneficial, but also necessary; and that were labor to cease the world would stagnate and become wholly demoralized. He should show that labor is not degrading, but instead that it is elevating, and that it is in reality **a** blessing. The judicious teacher can do much in correcting the wrong notions of boys in this respect, and in leading them to look on education as something more than mere textbook drudgery.

17. Having too Many Classes.—This is an error which is likely to exist mostly in the ungraded school, and it is one difficult to avoid where the school is overcrowded. In a school of ordinary size, however, the true economy is to have as few classes as possible. Age, capacity, and size of classes ought all to be considered in making the permanent classification of the school. If the school is too large, then it will be best to alternate the recitations of some of the classes, hearing them recite only every other day. When the class has no recitation for the day, let them still have their period of study, and let them prepare their work on slates or on the blackboard, or even write it out on paper for the teacher's inspection. Recitations, however, should be so arranged that every one may have something to do each day; otherwise the pupils will soon lose interest and the work of the teacher will be fruitless.

18. Having too Many Rules and Regulations.—The teacher should not go into the school-room with a list of rules and regulations prepared. Let rules be adopted only when the necessity for them arises. The wise plan is for the teacher to say nothing about rules until the behavior of the pupils makes it necessary to put some in force, and then the plan heretofore suggested should be used in their adoption. The fewer the rules the less difficult will be the work of government, because the fewer will be the violations.

The great work of the teacher ought to be teaching, not keeping an orderly school. Pupils ought to be well-behaved, and restrictions and rules ought to be for the check of those only who are not inclined to do right. It ought not to be expected of the teacher that he spend any great part of his time in keeping order. Imagine the new minister of a parish, when he takes charge of a congregation, first laying down a set of rules with regard to whispering, laughing, shuffling of feet, leaving seats, etc. during sermon, and then imagine him, while delivering that sermon, stopping occasionally to preserve order. It would be something unprecedented, and yet, barring the thoughtlessness of children, there ought to be no more reason for adopting rules in the one case than there ought in the other.

19. Giving too Little Attention to Manners and Morals. —The teacher himself ought to be a person whose manners and personal character are worthy of imitation by his pupils; but, independent of this, he ought to give frequent instruction in an informal way on the subject of good manners and correct morals. Much may be done by reading anecdotes to the children—much also by reading to them such stories as are found in Cowderry's *Moral Lessons*, each of which illustrates some positive moral virtue in such a way as to make it interesting and easily comprehended by children. Excellent advice may also be gathered from Gow's *Good Morals and Gentle Manners*, a practical book on the etiquette of every-day life which all pupils can appreciate. The teacher should frequently read or relate stories illustrating both morals and manners. The pupils will draw their own conclusions, and in every instance some one will be touched

and a good effect be wrought. Bain says, "A moral lesson may be wrapped up in a tale and brought home with an impetus. Stories of great and noble deeds have fired more youthful hearts with enthusiasm than sermons have."

An excellent plan is for the teacher to keep a scrap-book, into which he should gather from time to time such suitable anecdotes and stories as he may meet with in his reading. They will always be found a convenient medium by which to convey practical instruction in both morals and manners. He should give advice also, as opportunity may occur, in the choice of reading matter, selecting at all times interesting and healthful books. He ought under no circumstances, however, to mention offensive books and caution pupils against reading them. Next to advertising by praise, nothing is more effective than advertising by condemnation. Let pupils be cautioned against reading certain books as demoralizing in their character, and there will always be a large percentage who will search out the condemned books and read them for the mere gratification of curiosity.

20. Giving too Little Attention to Physical Culture.— With most pupils but little difficulty will be experienced in the matter of exercise. Nature has implanted in the human constitution that same desire to play which is characteristic of the young of all animal kind. But children in school will gradually fall into habits which may prove quite as harmful as the neglect of exercise, and to these the teacher must give strict attention. They include improper and ungraceful postures in both sitting and standing, reading and studying with deficient or too strong light, sitting in an uncomfortable room, studying

so intensely as to cause headache, eating at irregular times, lunching between meals, going out of doors without sufficient protection ; and in fact all that may be embraced under the head of violations of hygienic laws.

It is vastly better that pupils should have correct hygienic habits and a thorough knowledge of their own physical being than that they should have a knowledge of all the other sciences of a school course. Horace Mann, one of America's greatest educators, says: "At college I was taught the motions of the heavenly bodies, as if their keeping in their orbits depended on my knowing them, while I was in profound ignorance of the laws of health of my own body. The rest of my life was in consequence one long battle of exhausted energies." This, too, would be the testimony of most great scholars—not that mental discipline and hard study do harm, but that the neglect of physical culture, and the training of the mind at the expense of health, are injurious in the extreme.

21. Giving too Much Help.—The mind, like the body, grows stronger by exercise, and the best and most profitable exercise is that which the child gets from his own work. The teacher does the child a great wrong in doing his work for him. The more a pupil does for himself, the greater will be his self-dependence and the more thorough his mental discipline. As well might we expect a child to grow physically strong if continually carried in the nurse's arms, as expect him to grow mentally strong while receiving the constant help of the teacher. It is what the child does for himself that strengthens his mental faculties and fits him for his subsequent work.

The pupil should not be permitted, however, to waste time in wrestling with difficulties beyond his strength. He should have no direct help in doing that which he can do for himself; but it is useless and unprofitable to permit him to waste time in attempting to solve problems beyond his comprehension. When the teacher once discovers that the child is unable to overcome a difficulty, it is then time for him to give such suggestions as will start a proper train of thought in the mind of the child, and thus enable him to win the victory.

22. Assuming that Parents and Directors are the Teacher's Enemies.—It is a great mistake for teachers to assume that both the patrons and the Directors are their natural enemies; and this mistake has caused in many schools a great degree of difficulty which might have been avoided to the advantage of both teacher and pupils. When once fully convinced that the teacher is working for the best interests of the school, no one naturally feels a greater desire to promote the success and progress of the pupils than does the parent. Why should he be an enemy? Certainly it is to his advantage that his own children make proper progress in their studies, and that he give the teacher such encouragement as will lead him to work honestly and faithfully for the best development of the children under his control.

But should the teacher know that both patrons and Directors are unfavorable to him at first, he should not for a moment show that he believes such to be the fact. Every effort should be made to win them over—first, by his good work in the school; and, second, by his being genial, pleasant, polite, and sociable when he meets them. If he manifests this kind of spirit toward them, he need have little fear of the final result.

23. **The too Rapid Introduction of Reforms.** —It is never wise to attempt sudden changes or reforms on taking charge of a school. A teacher may find many things in his own work or in that of his predecessor which he thinks ought to be otherwise, but he should proceed very cautiously if a change is to be made. If improved methods are desirable, let him first convince those whom these methods most concern as to their value and importance. If he once secures their assistance and co-operation, the reform can readily be made; but if he must make it against their opposition, it is better for him to endure the evils which already exist than invite those whose magnitude he may find still greater.

24. **Casting Reflections on One's Predecessor.** — The teacher should be cautious not to make unfriendly remarks with reference to his predecessor, nor should he by either word or manner encourage his pupils to indulge in such remarks. His predecessor may have made very serious mistakes, but the wiser plan will be for the teacher to show these by the excellence of his own work rather than, by calling attention to them.

A very serious fault of this same nature is that of a teacher's showing his lack of confidence in the work of his predecessor by turning all back to the beginning of the book. The custom is still a very general one in most ungraded schools. It would be much better to start where their previous teacher ended his instruction, or at most turn back a few pages only, so that they may not be discouraged. If their teaching has been defective

24 *

it will soon become manifest, and both teacher and pupils can then agree upon a plan which will make the instruction more effective.

25. Making Excuses to Visitors.—This sort of complaint is usually made with the design of impressing upon the minds of visitors that the teacher could do very much better work if he only had a chance—that is, if the Directors were better educated and could appreciate good teaching, if the parents were not so ignorant and prejudiced, if the school-house were more desirably located, if the teacher had a better supply of apparatus, if the preceding teacher had not spoiled the school, if the pupils were not so stupid, and so on.

A teacher of this kind never looks at his own work for the cause of failure. He would not for a moment admit that it is his own deficiency that he is trying to excuse in making these charges upon everybody else. What he should do is, make the best of the situation and do as well as he can, leaving the judgment as to his work to the decision of others.

26. A Lack of Enthusiasm.—Enthusiasm makes the successful teacher. All the learning in the world will not win success in the school-room for the lazy teacher. President Chadbourne says: "Without enthusiasm no teacher can have the best success, however learned and faithful and hard-working he may be. Enthusiasm is the heat that softens the iron, that every blow may tell. Enthusiasm on the part of the teacher gives life to the student and an impulse to every mental power. When this is accomplished, there is no more waste in lifting, dragging, or driving. It was the enthusiasm of Agassiz that clothed the commonest things with new life and

beauty—that charmed every listener, and transformed the aged and the young, the ignorant and the learned, into joyful learners."

27. Discouraging Pupils.—Dr. Arnold of Rugby says that he never was so ashamed as when, after giving a boy a sharp reproof, the latter turned to him and said, " Why do you speak angrily, sir ? Indeed, I am doing the best I can." Pupils should be praised rather than discouraged. Many of them think but slowly, and the teacher will need, therefore, to exercise great patience with their seeming stupidity and dullness. Many a teacher overshoots the mark in his teaching because what to him may be very easy is difficult for his pupils. This in itself greatly discourages them, and when, in addition to this, he complains of their inability to meet his expectations, the burden becomes to them doubly grievous. Let him bring his teaching down to their level, correct his own faults, and praise where praise is due, and both he and the pupils will be the better for it.

28. Wounding the Feelings of Children.—The teacher should be cautious to make no remarks that are likely to hurt the feelings of his pupils. It is not only unwise, but also unkind, to refer to them as numskulls, dunces, and the like. Nor should the teacher compare his pupils with one another. The only result of such comparison, when expressed before others, is to create antagonism between the parties compared, and no possible benefit can result from the practice.

29. Being Arbitrary.—The teacher should not assume that he is the only one interested in the work in which he is engaged, and therefore he should not arbitrarily decide every question as it may arise without consultation

with those whose business it is to supervise the school work. Many a teacher has brought trouble on himself by assuming the rights and duties of both teacher and Directors. Nor should the teacher be arbitrary in his treatment of pupils. Obedience will be secured much more readily when the pupils see the justice and appreciate the reasonableness of his demands. No one is so liable as the teacher to become dogmatic and opinionated. The very nature of his calling and his associations and surroundings are such as to produce this result.

30. **Gloominess.**—Few are so repulsive to child-nature as those who are gloomy. The teacher who is stiff and pedantic, who is sullen and morose, who is gloomy and dejected, is out of place in the school-room. Child-life is joyous and cheerful, and no man or woman has any right to throw clouds and shadows around it; much less should such a person act as teacher. None but those of a cheerful temperament should enter upon the work of teaching.

The teacher will find many things to try his patience, many things to vex and cross him, many things that will discourage and irritate him; but through it all let him keep a cheerful countenance. Let him join in a hearty laugh whenever there is an opportunity. No one needs more to look on the bright side of life. Some one has said, " Whatever temper you have suffered to grow up to the gradual habit of years, that will get a daily revelation over your desks as visible as any maps on the walls." If that habit be one of gloominess, what must be the unfortunate influence on the children!

Teacher, cultivate a cheerful disposition and a pleasant countenance. You will relieve your work of half the difficulties by which it is surrounded. Let your entrance into the school-room be such as to convince your pupils that you are both good-humored and good-natured. Goldsmith expressed more philosophy than he dreamed of in his description of the schoolmaster of "sweet Auburn:"

> "A man severe he was, and stern to view;
> I knew him well, and every truant knew.
> Well had the boding tremblers learned to trace
> The day's disasters in his morning face."

Let the effort of every teacher's life be to avoid furnishing the text for a similar quatrain by some future Goldsmith.

THE END.

Lightning Source UK Ltd.
Milton Keynes UK
UKOW05f2354131216
289968UK00015B/503/P